WHAT

STAYING HEALTHY AND WHOLE

ABOUT

(WHILE YOU'RE HELPING OTHERS)

ME?

RENÉE HILL CARTER

Featuring conversations with Dr. Samuel R. Chand and others

What About Me?
Staying Healthy and Whole (While You're Helping Others)
by Renée Hill Carter

copyright ©2019
ISBN: 978-1-943294-94-7

cover design by Kiryl Lisenko

What About Me? is available in Amazon Kindle, Barnes & Noble Nook and Apple iBooks.

CONTENTS

DEDICATION

To my husband, Bill, my partner and the love of my life always. Ours is an amazing love story from that day in 1969 to now that only God could write so masterfully.

To my children, William Keith, Jr., LaKeshia, and LaChanda. It's difficult to find the words that adequately describe my love for you. I am by the grace of God, blessed and highly favored to be your mother.

To my son-in-law, Mitchell, and my grandchildren. You are a blessing to my daughter, LaKeshia, and to my amazing grand-children, Mitchell, Jr. and Kamryn. Thank you for loving them so. I love you all.

To my dear sister, Georgianna, who is truly my best friend. The bond we share is indescribable. I love you and I thank God for you always.

And to other family members I know and love and those I did not have the privilege to know from my home of origin, I dedi-cate this book to you.

ACKNOWLEDGEMENTS

M Y SINCERE GRATITUDE to all who so graciously gave to this endeavor. (Listed in alphabetical order.)

Dr. Samuel R. Chand

Dr. Mark A. Croston

Dr. Gina Newsome Duncan

Mrs. Rita K. Garnto

Mrs. Renita K. Hopkins

Bishop Joey Johnson

Dr. Ramona Joseph

Mr. Gilbert & Dr. Barbara L. Peacock

Dr. Rob & Dr. Karla Robinson

Ms. Natasha Stewart

Thank you for taking the time to talk with me and share your skills, passions, gifts, and some tender places from your heart. Your authenticity, transparency, and love for the souls that God has entrusted to your care are evident. I appreciate your patience, too. You understand and embrace the fact that caring for your own soul is a mark of divine health as God intended. It is clear that your motivation is the love you have for your God. I appreciate each of you from the depths of my heart.

In addition to those whose conversations are featured, I am deeply grateful to Dr. Larry Crabb for the gift of his book, *A Different Kind of Happiness*. Your words help me to see "above the sun" in a different light.

My gratitude to all the women I was privileged to chat with whether at coffee, lunch, text, email, church, conferences, Bible studies, etc. You shared your feelings, your concerns, your challenges, and your heart. Accept my prayers and gratitude for the good work God has begun in you. Hopefully, we'll talk more.

To Kathy Green, my publishing consultant. What a Godsend you are. Your expertise, keen eye, patience, and wisdom are priceless. The fact that you are gifted as a passionate *prayer* and author is a divine bonus.

To all who encouraged me with your kind words and gentle (and sometimes not so gentle) nudges to turn my thesis into this book, I am eternally grateful.

Some people build fences to keep people out, and other people build fences to keep people in.

–*Fences*, by August Wilson

FOREWORD

WHAT ABOUT ME?" is a valid question, which deserves a valid response. For years, Christian leaders of all denominations have suffered silently due to the fear of rejection or being publicly disgraced, or perhaps they had no one to confide in or trust with their deepest struggles and greatest needs. All too often leaders fail to receive the personal care that is required to maintain optimal health and wholeness while tending to the needs of others. As a result, their needs have gone unmet and many have reached the point of no return.

God's ears are not dull of hearing the cries of His people who yearn for someone to notice their pain and relieve their aching hearts and troubled minds. Especially those us of who are called to the front lines of battle. The heart of God longs for His people to walk in complete wholeness with nothing missing and nothing broken. This is why He sent Jesus to earth to shed His precious blood. When God searched the earth for someone to fill in the gap and make up the hedge on behalf of Christian leaders, Renée Hill Carter responded, "Here I am, Lord. Send me!"

As a Prayer Author, Teacher, and Publishing Consultant, I share Renée's passion to minister to the needs of the afflicted. For this reason, from the moment I first spoke with her about writing and publishing her book, I knew I had to do whatever I could to assist her with bringing forth this message. It has been an absolute privilege to serve as Renée's publishing consultant on this project. I admire her compassionate heart and the great courage she has shown by tackling this assignment in the spirit of excellence. Renée has refused to stand idle or look the other way, but through her book she has broken the silence on this vital topic.

Raising the subject of who will attend to the care and well-being of our leaders, Renée recognizes the magnitude of this concern. She is a woman of integrity who has devoted years of her life to research this topic as well as converse with influential Christian leaders, including pastors, licensed counselors and therapists, and other health care professionals to bring forth the wisdom and knowledge which is shared in this book. You will find their conversations deeply compelling and insightful.

"What About Me?" is an invaluable tool that will offer hope and healing to all who suffer behind the scenes of ministry. I congratulate you, Renée Hill Carter on a job well done. The Bible tells us, "For God is not unjust. He will not forget how hard you have worked for him and how you have shown your love to him by caring for other believers, as you still do" (Hebrews 6:10 NLT). May God use this message around the globe to transform the lives of His people for His glory.

Kathy R. Green
Publishing Consultant
KathyRGreen.com

INTRODUCTION

H OW YOU FEELIN'?" That was Todd's standard greeting. We worked together on staff at my church. It didn't matter who or where or when, I always knew I would hear this greeting from our then Head of School at the Male Leadership Academy. I imagine as we both moved to our next assignments, a physical move for him and me by way of retirement, his brand of hello remained. And so I ask, "How you feelin'?" It actually offers a clear precedent as to what this book is about.

What About Me? emerged from my thesis for the Master of Christian Counseling degree. Written in 2007 with a focus on the emotional health primarily of pastors and spiritual leaders in the church and faith community, it was aptly titled, *The Biblical Counselor: A Healthy Profile of the Soul Care Provider in the 21st Century Church.*

A mouthful, I know, but that's what a thesis is, a lot of words of thought to prove a point. And, let's be clear, I was on a mission to fulfill the requirements to get that degree I had worked so hard for!

It wasn't easy. I began my studies in 1999, graduated with my class in 2004 but did not get the piece of paper signifying my completion until three years later in 2007. The death of my mother in 2003 and then my oldest sister in 2005 plunged me into the depths of grief that stilled my pen to baby strokes at best.

I found life and strength to finish my work in 2007. After breathing a long sigh of relief (I did get an "A" by the way), I proudly put the bound copy on the shelf. I was done or so I thought.

WHAT ON EARTH IS GOING ON?

Although my thesis writing days were over, life continued at a sometimes feverish pitch. The sudden death of the senior pastor of my church threw not only me but an entire congregation and so many others in his sphere of influence into an emotional whirlwind of grief.

Life marched on often leaving me with the question, "what on earth is going on?" You may have asked the same question. The normal events of living that sometimes stir the emotions of the human soul to a boiling overflow have no limits, no boundaries and no particular favorites. Attempts to keep things at bay and within your control are futile. Feelings and emotions that come with birth, death, divorce, civil disobedience, sin, illnesses temporary and terminal, hatreds seen and unseen, bad things happening to good people; good things happening to bad people cannot be denied and are intrinsic to all five senses, like it or not.

The walls of our institutions of government, education, business, media, sports, arts and entertainment, family and religion are broken down. Efforts to rebuild are hampered by the rubbish of greed, idolatry and hedonism yet the mandate to repair and build up those affected remains.

And then it seems that all the *normal* events of life have taken on a different persona, at least in my lifetime. We're experiencing a heightened alert produced by atrocities that previously were scarcely heard of, but have somehow settled into a horrific almost daily routine. Mass murders, school shootings, video footage of the death of a mother's child with the world as a witness bombard us. The blatant display of good being called evil and evil being called good, make breaking news commonplace. A proliferation of physical and mental assaults on the mind, body and spirit whether sexual, racial, or verbal, denigrates the human condition to a state of hatred, mistrust and retaliation. It's personal and recovery is slow or sometimes not at all.

We continually experience groaning not only in our soul but also in the earth. As of this writing, two hurricanes gripped the east coast in quick succession allowing no break to catch our breath and recover. We stare at the TV screen in disbelief at splintered homes resembling pick up sticks; the distraught search for where houses once stood strong; loved ones battered in mind, body and spirit. In some cases life was cut short, death prevailed without the courtesy of a warning.

Raging fires of devastation are ravaging the west coast. The effects of global warming touch all points in between and beyond with other extreme, unpredictable and out of order weather events. The tsunami waters were too much for one side but not enough to quench the fires on the other side of our land.

Just as the earth drowns, burns and quakes, our whole being might follow suit. Emotional upheaval has spiked throughout the world producing fears of mammoth proportion. Personal calamity lays siege on our body producing stress and dis-ease. Our desire for happiness, peace and goodwill on earth is sabotaged testing even our faith.

HOLISTIC HEALTH AND WELL-BEING: PHYSICAL, SPIRITUAL AND MENTAL

Our beings created for perfection are not so perfect and somewhat fractured because of the disorder in our world. Every part of our being at some time or another is subject to a disparaging health diagnosis. Our physical, spiritual and mental wellbeing are at stake and need focused attention. In some cases, thought patterns are disturbed, imbalanced or tangled in disarray. Reactions to the cacophony of less than desirable events vary from person to person but can manifest under the broad label of mental illness. We can be hesitant to openly discuss this subject particularly when it hits home. Sometimes it's treated as taboo and not to be talked about period. Yet, mental illness insists on showing up in the least likely of families, at the most inconvenient time and wants to convince us that the brain and the mind are somehow not at all related and not a likely target in the whole scheme of who we are.

The goal of holistic health which includes the mental aspect is breaking its silence. The essence of who we are must now speak in unison to respect and honor God's marvelous handiwork. He created us whole and complete in His image. Our voice should reflect a desire to be conformed as such. Neglect and looking the other way are no longer viable options. For where there's emotional debris in one part of the house, all the rooms will sooner or later experience a pile-up of anxiety, depression, psychotic disorders and even suicidal thoughts with completion. Mental hoarding is like physical hoarding not visible to the naked eye but nonetheless screams for help and can no longer be muffled.

THE SEARCH

To appease the cries of a debilitated soul, the mind will sometimes go on a reconnaissance. To get rid of the pain, a fruitless search and destroy mission ensues. Addictions mimic relief in a deceptive way while the soul is found wanting still. To close the gaping wound in the heart, opioids and even social media are now added to the overcrowded list of numbing agents and behaviors. The globe has morphed into a community shaped by social media in sometimes unhealthy ways. Truth be told, we all are affected. Our children are affected. Our elderly are affected. More Truth. God told us to expect emotional, physical, and spiritual distressing trials, nevertheless the feelings they generate are real. When we taste them, we are sick to the stomach of our souls and often ill prepared to pursue healing. Those who are affected need help to process the pain. Those they go to (or look for) need help to process it, too. And if that's not enough, the greater culprit, as the eternal and all wise God also informed us, "because lawlessness will abound, the love of many will wax cold." (Matt. 24:12 KJV)

A WELFARE CHECK FOR SOULS WHO CARE

As the longing and troubled souls come for help, the lives of "soul care providers" as I call them, experience the same troubles. Expectations to give hope that will calm and settle the queasiness of fear, angst and hopelessness are great. What happens to these souls that are appointed to do the caring? What is the welfare and health of their soul? Do we trivialize the feelings that the death of a loved one brings with well-rehearsed spiritual platitudes even for them? And what about divorce; the pain of a severed relationship that you're told to get over; the news you get that sends awry the dreams that you so carefully carved out for your future or for your child; or the carnage of sin that has consciously or unconsciously become an insidious game of hide and seek. What should we do with the sinking feeling that slowly resembles complacency or apathy after a whopping serving from social media and the all-day and all night news channels? How do we respond when we want to pray, to praise, to do what we know to do, but can't. Resignation is a virus designed to take us all out if we're not *care-filled* not only for their souls but for our own.

Jesus guaranteed us in John 16:33, that in this world we will have tribulation (Point A), but to be of good cheer because He has overcome the world.(Point B). Some of us can get from point A to point B rather quickly, but others need help because a process is involved. I believe, but I can't move; I'm stuck. I'm on an exhausting, loopy treadmill and can't seem to make progress. How do I move from utter devastation to joyful victory without glaring judgement from within and without?

This trek is typically the road less traveled. The inward journey of the soul is usually littered with detour signs. Barricades to avoid the danger ahead directs us another way. Aren't we curious though as to what is around the bend? What are we avoiding? What if it leads to another disaster; a sinkhole? Suppose the shoulders are washed away and should we skid off the road, how will we get back on track?

Or what if these are imaginary barricades that either we created or were created for us long ago by someone from our home of origin?

The road less traveled is sometimes dark and unpredictable yet hidden treasures of peace, relief and release are often just waiting to be discovered

WHAT THIS BOOK IS NOT

What About Me? is not an indictment but is an opportunity to incite or fuel more conversations, considerations, convictions and confessions. In turn, responsibility to actively and decisively improve and draw more attention to the emotional and mental health of those who provide soul care will hopefully be realized. Change is a plausible outcome.

WHAT THIS BOOK IS

What About Me? can easily fit into the "self-help" genre. Intended to be a self-help book of sorts, a more inclusive fit is "self-health" for the soul. You're invited to listen in on conversations with friends and colleagues in the faith about personal soul care. As soul care providers, they are experiencing and grasping on a continual basis the value and the mandate from God to holistically guard their health—spirit, soul and body. You will hear personal stories and lessons learned through study, work, relationships, life experiences, and even relate to their pains and joys of living. You'll feel with them and overhear conversations from intimate moments with their God.

I am grateful for their honesty, authenticity, transparency and wisdom that they bring to the table. Their thoughts and even suggestions are worth considering. What you read will summon you and challenge you to go to the next level of holistic self-care, growth and development. Perhaps a more conscious interconnectivity of spirit, soul and body is warranted. This book will amplify what I believe is the most neglected part of us. It will challenge the often dismissive attitude towards our **soul**—the place where our emotions, our will, our heart, our decision making, and yes, our feelings live.

I don't want to tell you how to read this book. We all have our own style of reading. All I ask (and pray) is that as you read, God's purpose is fulfilled. The goal is that something said is stimuli towards you embracing and doing better when it comes to your emotional and mental health and wellbeing. Whether you agree or not, let something you hear be a catalyst to unsettle you and enlighten a different and better place of thinking about your soul and each soul that God sends your way. Both souls, theirs and yours are delicate, hand crafted and delivered on a priceless platter by the Soul Maker Himself. Take care to take care.

What About Me? is formatted in a unique way. It contains conversations over a period of time beginning in April 2007 and ending in October 2018. Each chapter is a conversation beginning with a profile of the participants. My friends were asked to focus on particular aspects of holistic self-care that inform the health of the soul. Nestled between chapters, you'll see inserts from me noted by, "Meditational Soul Note". The tone will vary. You might find excerpts of thought from other authors and colleagues; my thoughts; excerpts from my thesis and other writings, and God's thoughts from the Bible. At the end of each chapter are opportunities for you to ponder: Considerations, Confessions, Convictions, and More Conversations. Should *Change* be activated as a result, "Yay you!" (You'll see this later).

WHO THIS BOOK IS FOR

Written unashamedly from a Christian perspective, this book is for you, regardless of your faith, your religion, your beliefs, your profession, your gender, your race or ethnicity. The only requirement is that you have a soul that cares.

It is for anyone whose soul is typically a "go to" place for hope, for answers, for leadership, to get a listening heart with ears when nobody else will hear. It is also for those who are in need of their help.

The Soul Care Providers list is exhaustive and difficult to be conclusive. Although *What About Me?* is written with a viewpoint of those in specific professions and ministry/serving areas of health, the principles are widely useful and applicable regardless of titles or professions. It can include but not limited to School Counselors and Educators, Spiritual and Faith leaders, School coaches, College Chaplains, Attorneys, Hospice workers and Grief Counselors; Therapists, Health Care Professionals, Parents, Missionaries; CEO's, Social Workers; Law Enforcement; First Responders; Caregivers for aging parents, a sick spouse, a sick child; for anybody you love. (Add yourself to the list if you're not on it)

One thing we will agree on is the desire for a prosperous and healthy soul. I hope you'll find something along the way to consider that you can change for the better. Make God proud that He made you, fearfully and wonderfully for such time as this.

Now, step back, take a deep breath and take the time to honestly ask yourself "How you feelin'?"

CHAPTER 1

A HEALTHY PROFILE OF A SOUL CARE PROVIDER IN THE 21ST CENTURY CHURCH

In Conversation with *Dr. Samuel R. Chand*

WHO WOULD HAVE thought, when in 1973 "student" Sam Chand was serving Beulah Heights Bible College as janitor, cook, and dishwasher that he would return in 1989 as "President" of the same college! Under his leadership, it became the country's largest predominantly African-American Christian College.

Sam Chand is a former Pastor, college President, and Chancellor, and now serves as President Emeritus of Beulah Heights University.

As a Dream Releaser, Sam Chand serves Pastors, ministries, and businesses as a Leadership Architect and Change Strategist. Sam Chand has served as senior Pastor, college President, Chancellor, and President Emeritus.

He personally consults, mentors, and coaches some of the country's largest churches' Pastors, and speaks regularly at leadership conferences, churches, corporations, Leadership Roundtables, Minister's Conferences, seminars, and other leadership development opportunities. He was named in the top-30 global leadership gurus list.

Sam Chand develops leaders through Leadership Consultations and Leadership Resources—books/CDs and Leadership Speaking. Leaders are using Sam Chand's books as handbooks worldwide in leadership development.

Being raised in a pastor's home in India has uniquely equipped Sam Chand to share his passion—that of mentoring, developing, and inspiring leaders to break all limits—in ministry and the marketplace.

In this season of his life, Sam Chand does one thing—Leadership. His singular vision for his life is to "Help Others Succeed." (www.samchand.com).

[BEGINNING OF CONVERSATION PART 1, APRIL 13, 2007]

Renée: You are a consultant and an expert in the area of leadership. Tell me a little about who you are and what you do.

Dr. Chand: I'm a product of a whole lot of different things. I was born and raised in a pastor's home in India, and so I have that heart for pastors and I started to notice that there are not a whole lot of resources for pastors to tap into personally and individually. One thing led to the other, and I ended up serving pastors and that's all I do. I want to be a pastor's best friend and make their life the most effective while they are on this planet.

Renée: You serve pastors. You were a pastor at one point.

Dr. Chand: Yes I was before the Lord set me free *(laughter)*. I did pastor for a season. I was Assistant Pastor at three churches and then I was Senior Pastor of one church.

Dr. Sam Chand

Renée: How long ago was that?

Dr. Chand: That was in 1989 when I transitioned from pastoring. I was a senior pastor for nine years at one church.

Renée: Am I correct that you have a Master's Degree in Christian Counseling?

Dr. Chand: My Master's is in Biblical Counseling from Grace Theological Seminary in Winona Lake, IN.

Renée: And you also had some well-known professors, I believe.

Dr. Chand: I did—Dr. Larry Crabb was my mentor. I also learned a great deal from Dr. Dan Allender and Dr. Tom

Varney who write a lot on this subject. There have been many good people in my life.

Renée: How valuable was that degree to you when you began to pastor?

Dr. Chand: It was very valuable in the sense that I didn't understand the complexity of the human nature and that some things take time. I was the normal pastor that when someone brings you a problem, let me fix it for you, let me pray with you, and then you go home, and it's solved. As I understood process and people, I learned that good healing comes in the context of relationships and what that is all about. It broadened a lot of things that I had no idea about.

Renée: Would you say that many pastors don't have a counseling educational background?

Dr. Chand: Most pastors don't. I think that most pastors by nature are care providers, nurturers—they have the best interest at heart for people. They are wise people called of God and want people to live healthy whole lives. So God does give them wisdom in the midst of all that. But to say that they have a counseling background, counseling training, that's not true of most pastors.

Renée: In the work that you do all over the country with pastors and other church leaders, do you see that as perhaps a hindrance to them being willing to embrace the responsibility of counseling in the church, or am I being too presumptuous?

Dr. Chand: I think you can counsel people as long as there is a church of about 150 people, but after that, it starts breaking down because there are so many more critical things that need to be handled in the church. Pastors need to ask themselves the question, "What are things that only I can do in the church?" Counseling is one of those things that others can do, and so he has many options as to how he can respond to that.

Renée: Would you say that typically when pastors do not feel equipped to counsel and there is no one trained in the church, they leave the counseling to secular therapists, or is there a trend now of embracing counsel for the souls of God's people back to the church?

Dr. Chand: There is a definite shift there. First of all, there are prepared people that are available to the church. Churches have embraced the importance of it, so they allocate personnel, resources, and space for counseling. I know many churches that have full-time counselors on staff. There are so many more resources than there were earlier.

Renée: When you did counsel, do you feel that you were a healthy counselor?

Dr. Chand: I don't know if I am ever fully healthy.

Renée: What does it take to be healthy?

Dr. Chand: I don't think anyone is ever fully healthy. I think we all have that dysfunctional side to us and sometimes we can overcome it, but we all deal with our mess on an ongoing basis. Healthy to me means being able to help somebody and ready to do it selflessly, not selfishly or having anything to prove. So when I was counseling, I had tinges of health from time to time and a lot of unhealth, so it helps to identify the inmates of the asylum *(laughter)*. It's a mixed bag.

Renée: Did you have a counselor?

Dr. Chand: Yes, in fact when my wife and I got married, we both agreed that if something was to go wrong in the marriage, who we would counsel with. And yes, I've had a number of counselors in my life.

Renée: Do you think that contributes to your health?

Dr. Chand: I think that every counselor needs a counselor. Just like every pastor needs a pastor. Therapists will tell you that every therapist is in therapy themselves because there is so much being brought to you constantly. There is no way you can take in all of what comes to you in the counseling environment, usually negativity or depression or pessimism, hopelessness or helplessness or abuse, and somehow not start being affected by it. So every counselor needs a counselor.

Renée: You're taking it all in and you need to let it out.

Dr. Chand: You need to be able to debrief.

Renée: Can you share a particular instance when your personal life affected you being able to properly counsel, and what did you do?

Dr. Chand: Well, there were times when my wife and I were having issues, and I knew that would not be a good time for me to be counseling people. So if I had a counseling appointment and something was going on in my home, I would have the office call and say something has come up and we'd have to reschedule because that's a vulnerable moment. There are times when personal issues get in the way. If I am already disappointed in that person, or I'm already ticked off at them on a totally different subject and now they've come to talk to me about something, I'm having a hard time hearing them. If somebody else has found out that they are coming to counseling and they say, "Pastor, before they come in for counseling, you may want to know this." So now, all that background noise camouflages because in counseling, I've got to engage with *you* and hear *you*. But when I've got all the other voices, it's hard to hear *you*—it's hard to see *you* for what you're trying to present.

Renée: How long did it take you to identify those moments and be wise enough to make a decision not to deal with that person at that moment? Is that a process of learning?

Dr. Chand: It's a process of learning and growing and hearing what others are saying, "I don't do this and I always do this." You glean the best practices from people around you. You learn to ask yourself when I am the most vulnerable or when I'm the least effective. *Timing* is critical to everything. Those are not rules you make, but you grow into.

Renée: So that would be good advice for young pastors?

Dr. Chand: I hope so, because you want to go out there when you are halfway up on your game, and not if you are going through a depression time, for example. Most pastors go through a depressive swing on Sunday afternoon through Monday. It's just how it is when you're around people and they suck the energy out of you. When you've given all you can give, that's a time when you're the most vulnerable, so you know it's not the best time to counsel.

Renée: You have to be true to yourself.

Dr. Chand: You have to be true to acknowledging that you have the weak times, and it's not just weak morally or ethically, it's just that you don't have it to give.

Renée: It's being human.

Dr. Chand: That's right, and you have to replenish your energies.

Renée: During your down times, what would be your advice to that pastor? What resources should he or she have at their disposal to accommodate those times?

Dr. Chand: If there are occasional down times, that's one thing. But if there are chronic down times, then you need professional help—I think strengthening your family relationships and being healthy in your inner walk with the Lord. Being aware that the thing that you're counseling about might be an issue that you need counseling yourself. I think it's *the* *authentic you that's the most powerful tool in counseling...the genuine you.*

Renée: It is important to have a healthy counseling system in place in your church, be it the utilization of lay leaders or deacons that the pastor has sanctioned to be a team. That's very important to have others trained who've been given the authority by the pastor to counsel.

Dr. Chand: That's an area in church that really gives the church a lot of legal exposure. Most states don't use the word 'counselor' or 'counseling' anymore. It could be 'lay helping,' and so I think that first of all, that the nomenclature of 'counselor' is not attached to a person. The other thing is if a pastor authorizes counselors, they've got to have adequate training, not just in counseling, but in referral skills. They've got to know that they're not a physician. They are only a physician's assistant and not a medical doctor. Even medical doctors know that they are not the surgeon. Those limits must be clear and defined and should include debriefing, keeping good records, breaking confidences in case of the threat of suicide, homicide or physical abuse. By law, it is a federal offense for not reporting those, even if there is suspicion. So I think that unless there is some real strong, ongoing training for counselors, just because someone's a deacon, I'd much rather have a non-deacon counselor rather than a deacon counselor.

Renée: Tell me more about that.

Dr. Chand: A deacon is a position—I'm dealing with a positional person here who's got authority and can hurt me if they wanted to. Any time a counselor represents authority, things get compromised and a deacon would probably do that for me. I wouldn't say they are 'deacons' who are counseling; I'd say they are just people who are helping.

Renée: And again—as you say it is semantics—it's the nomenclature of how you frame what you're doing.

Dr. Chand: Not all deacons can be counselors. It's not a deacon program—it is someone who happens to be a deacon. They are not a deacon counseling, but they're just a human being counseling.

Renée: So then, it's very important to have those outside systems in place. If that pastor recognizes the importance of having a system of helps for counseling, in soul care providing, then they will also have other Christian professionals that he can refer to.

Dr. Chand: Absolutely, I think that you can do some crisis counseling in-house—some low-level counseling.

Renée: Describe crisis counseling.

Dr. Chand: Crisis counseling would be death, bad news: "My wife's got cancer." Bad news would be, "My son just got picked up for DUI." Crisis counseling would be, "I'm ready to file bankruptcy." But that's just one time—I'd help them through it and refer them. I personally prefer training people in the house to do short-term counseling.

Renée: Solution-focused counseling.

Dr. Chand: Solution focused—no more than three sessions. Get them on track or at least have people in place that you refer to. So, you interview Christian counselors and see if they fit your worldview and your sense of ethics and say to them, "From time to time, we'll refer people to you," and let that be that.

Renée: Give instances of that type of referral.

Dr. Chand: Long-term marriage counseling, abuse...substance abuse or spousal abuse, depression, financial, nurturing issues, eating disorders like anorexia, mental issues. When people came with depression issues, mental issues, etc., I insisted that they get a physical, because sometimes it shows up as a chemistry issue, and people may not understand how one thing relates to the other.

Renée: Now, today we live in a postmodern era where there are no moral absolutes. How have the lives of people changed and their counseling needs changed as a result of that? How should the church respond?

Dr. Chand: Counseling is not the same as it used to be, obviously. Every time you are counseling, you're opening up, you're exposing; the counselor is saying, "Should I ask this question?" The other thing is that absolutes have moved, so some things we said we'd never allow have become a part of our mainstream culture.

Renée: Give an example.

Dr. Chand: An example would be the definition or redefinition of a family...it's acceptable, so the whole issue of absolutes in counseling becomes problematic. For example, the roles of husbands and wives have changed. In the old television series *Father Knows Best,* the husband goes to work and the wife stays home...all those things have continued to change. The only absolutes that we have are issues of righteousness and unrighteousness, rather than preferences. It used to be that the husband does this and the wife does this. That's really not true today. Needs have changed. A few years ago, there was a book called, *His Needs, Her Needs.* It's an interesting book and a very helpful book, but a very stereotypical book that all men have these five needs and all women have these five needs. So if that is your background and that becomes your absolute that she's a woman and she's got these five needs, she may not have those five needs. The only absolutes that I can approach are the black and white issues—righteousness and unrighteousness. If I'm clear that this is my preference, but if she does not do that, she's not going to hell.—I think that's where you ask if this is really Biblical or if this is something that I was raised with.

Renée: You are the author of the *Ladder* series, so obviously you promote—you teach, the team approach to ministry. I call it the "Jethro" approach to ministry in the church. Do pastors really embrace releasing certain responsibilities, or do they insist they are the only one that person can talk to?

Dr. Chand: I know very few pastors who enjoy counseling.

Renée: Why is that?

Dr. Chand: It really doesn't work for pastors. First of all, pastoral counseling is free and requires time. There can be 'no shows' because it's free.

Renée: In other words, it can be abused.

Dr. Chand: That's right. Then we've also found that people you help the most are the first to leave the church because there's the whole familiarity issue. It really boxes in the scope of pastoral preaching. If he does a lot of marriage counseling and then does a series on marriage, with any example he uses, someone's going to say, "He's talking about me." And, "Well, you can't talk to him because he's going to say it all from the pulpit." So pastors have found that they are good at other things and counseling bogs them down. So when pastors talk about that, I suggest to them that the only counseling they need to do is of their leaders—the elders, the deacons, the leadership team members. Everybody else either goes to a team inside the house who will do no more than three sessions and then after that, they are referred out to a Christian counselor or a Christian therapist. You can work out a deal on a sliding scale of payment. There are churches that consider counseling as a mission and will budget for it. They will provide a counselor on their campus. Let's say every Tuesday, Renée Carter will be there who's a credible, licensed practicing counselor, and if you cannot afford it, it is free or there's a sliding scale and the church will subsidize it. I know of a church that has a counselor on staff, and every staff member has a monthly counseling session with them. It is scheduled—it's automatic.

Renée: So there is a system in place.

Dr. Chand: Absolutely.

Renée: To summarize, give me your healthy profile of the soul care provider of today's church.

Dr. Chand: A healthy provider would be someone who is true to themselves, who would not approach a counseling session as having arrived, who would not talk down to people, who will be a collaborative force in their journey. Somebody who can share their own shortcomings and who has a sense of humor. They can laugh with people as they are going through their terrible times. A healthy soul care provider is somebody who is engaged in their own health on a constant basis. You don't have to have it together to help other people.

Renée: That can be freeing.

Dr. Chand: That is very freeing. Healthy soul care providers are people who understand the whole concept of holistic health. Healthy providers are people who have enough margin in their life to allow you to be dysfunctional and imperfect, and still love you. Healthy soul care providers are not demanding people, but they are people who are willing to let you work through your mess—not on their timetable, but on yours. Healthy soul care providers are people who can accept you where you are in life. So if I come to you and want to talk to you about my homosexuality, you will not push me away with "That is a sin." You'll end up talking about it I'm sure, but you will allow me to talk about my journey of molestation, abuse, and things that might have contributed to that and the shame that I feel. You will let me tell you about the broken relationships and my concerns with my personal health issues because of my exposure to that lifestyle.

You are an engaging counselor, not a judgmental counselor, but somebody who can walk with me wherever I am in life.

Renée: Someone who would counsel you as Jesus would.

Dr. Chand: That would be very nice.

Renée: Someone who would not be harder on you than God is on us.

Dr. Chand: That's right. I think a counselor is someone who ultimately gives hope to people; he doesn't fix them but says, "You can improve this." There's hope here.

Renée: Most of the time when someone comes to you, they're stuck. So perhaps a healthy counselor is one who can get that person unstuck and back on the road.

Dr. Chand: And I think another part of counseling is like your car where you have your scheduled maintenance. If you only took your car in for service when you had a problem, you wouldn't have a car very long. Just as you go for an annual physical, maintenance issues have to be addressed, as well. So counseling is not just for when you need it—maybe it's also when you don't need it.

Renée: So perhaps in a church environment, when there are resources, venues, opportunities available for people to be healthy, that will help the whole of counseling.

Dr. Chand: I think the emphasis is on health—not on "fixing it."

Renée: And maintenance is the key.

Dr. Chand: In every one of our bodies at any given time, there are unhealthy things going on. There are antibodies fighting against the issues going on in our life and in our world all the time. We are the dichotomy of healthy and unhealthy, but should constantly be working towards more healthy than unhealthy.

Renée: I'd like you to speak more about how counseling done by the pastor boxes in the scope of preaching.

Dr. Chand: It takes over the power of preaching. It affects the prophetic gift that the pastor has.

Renée: It derails it.

Dr. Chand: Absolutely—it makes preaching impotent. For example, you're getting ready to give an illustration, and you see *he's* right there and you think, "I can't say that." Or let's say somebody came and talked to you about embezzling funds or about their proclivity to 'varnish' the truth. Then in another session, someone confided in you about their suicidal thoughts. When you get up to preach, you might want to say, "You might be here this morning and feel like there's no hope for you," but you can't say that because of what *he* told me. You become constricted in your speaking about real life situations—you can hardly say anything. So the less I know about you, the more freedom I have to speak into your life.

Renée: That's why a system of counseling needs to be in place in the church.

Dr. Chand: Yes, and people need to know that these counselors don't tell me who is what, but there is a counseling director who does brief me regularly saying, "Pastor, our counseling load shows us that a lot of people are going through this." And you can even say [from the pulpit] that "my counseling team has told me that a number of you are dealing with these [issues] and that's why I want to preach the next three Sundays on this. But they have not given me any names, I have no idea, so let me look all around the room and say to all of you that you're all guilty *(laughter)*. I don't know *who,* but I do know *what.*" So that allows me to prepare my messages that are relevant; I can scratch where it is itching. So instead of being impotent, now you gain power from counselors.

Renée: Well Dr. Chand, again, I thank you so much.

Dr. Chand: It has been an honor to talk with you. Thank you.

[PART 2: NINE YEARS LATER...]

Renée Carter with Dr. Sam Chand and Brenda Chand

I caught up with Dr. Chand to find out how things are since we last spoke. So much life has happened, including personal challenges. He has consulted with so many more leaders, as well as stayed connected with those he's known over the years. Mrs. Chand was a part of our conversation this time, so let's listen in.

Renée: Nine years ago, you gave me your definition of a healthy soul care provider as someone who is engaged in their own health on a constant basis. So much has happened over the years. In your travels and your service to many, what have you observed about taking personal responsibility for soul care, particularly with pastors, chaplains, therapists, ministers, and ministry leaders in the church? How are they doing as far as their emotional and mental health is concerned?

Dr. Chand: A lot has changed in those years, as you well know. The stresses of life have changed, churches have changed, church folk have changed, and pastoring itself has changed. The world, the life that I was prepared for in Bible College and seminary does not exist anymore. Social media has changed, so now when people leave a church, they just don't leave the church, they post to everybody that they're leaving and why they are leaving. It's a continuum that takes its toll; however, there's also been quite a bit of moral crisis in the pulpit. People are more aware of the changes and things going on behind the scenes. People don't hold pastors up in the spotlight of esteem and I think that's good—very healthy. Some churches are prepared with restoration plans, and there are organizations now that do nothing but restore pastors.

People don't hold pastors up in the spotlight of esteem and I think that's good—very healthy.

I am working with a number of high-profile pastors who are going through it. There's a high level of depression, as well as high level of hope. I don't think that the train is moving in one direction, but in both directions simultaneously. With the constant changes in our world, we don't know what the future holds.

Renée: You mentioned that people don't hold pastors up in the spotlight of esteem, and you thought that's good—very healthy. Elaborate on that.

Dr. Chand: Let me clarify. I'm not supporting disrespect or dishonor of pastors. I'm seeing transparency and humanizing, that creates mutual trust and honesty. Health is knowing who you are and who you're not.

Renée: That's good to hear that pastors you've dealt with are responding to those changes. Can I safely say that they are willing to be vulnerable and to opening up to the fact that they don't have wings—that they are human and that they are seeking help and hope? How are they communicating that to the people they lead?

Dr. Chand: I think preaching has become much more transparent. Younger pastors are somewhat more transparent in their preaching. They are not out there preaching "all is well" like the previous generation has done a lot of times. They are willing to talk as much about the valleys, as well as the mountaintops. So there is a level of transparency that is flowing. There was a time where there were pat answers for everything—where problems had three proof texts and three scriptures. They fixed it, but that is not necessarily the case anymore. Pastors are coming to the pulpit a little better prepared with real-world experiences and real education experience. Churches are organizing. They are communicating on a whole different level. Marriages are a little bit more transparent. Younger wives have friends not only in the church, but outside of the church, as well. They are willing to talk about their challenges. Media, blogs, and other venues talk about challenges in ministry in a positive way. A lot is going on.

Renée: You mentioned that it appears younger pastors are more transparent and willing to speak more candidly from the pulpit about real issues because that's what people want to hear. They need to know that their pastor is human. What do we do about the older pastors who may not be there yet? How do we help them?

Dr. Chand: The only way that happens is when the older pastor goes through a tragedy to humanize them, to soften them. Their brokenness changes a lot of things. Preaching and hermeneutics changes their approach to the text. Brenda tells me that experience changes the paradigm.

Renée: Experience changes the paradigm. Thank you, Brenda! Dr. Chand, that sounds like something from your book, *Leadership Pain*. You talked about becoming a "pain partner" of some of the pastors. I interpret that as you're the soul care provider. What do you do with all the pain that's heaped upon you? How do you handle that in a healthy way?

Dr. Chand: When I started doing what I do, I knew that I would not be able to carry all that pain, so I asked for two gifts which I believe God gave me. One gift was simply favor, and by favor I mean being able to talk to pastors without having to go digging for information. When I sat down with them, they just opened up. Now unfortunately, I'm blessed with that gift, and it happens not just with pastors, but everywhere. People on airplanes, in hotels, the mall, talking about their money, their kids—it's crazy. They just tell me everything. The second gift I asked God for was detached concern, and He gave it to me. Detached concern means that when I'm with you, I'm 100 percent with you. I'm not checking my phone, but when I leave you, when I walk out of the office, when I get on the plane, I'm done.

I don't carry it with me. If you call me back, I pick up the phone, but I do not stay awake. I don't fret. I don't even follow through unless the pastor says, "Will you check up on me?" If they have a very important meeting coming up, or people's stuff is coming up, I just say to them: "Let me know," but the ownership has to be on them. It's a gift that I sought, and the Lord favored me with that.

Renée: That's wonderful. Now I'd like to shift to a personal challenge. You recently had a heart attack. How did you deal with the aftermath of that? Was that in any way associated with emotional or mental stress? Even though you have favor from God to be fully present as well as detached concern, you're still human. Tell me about that.

Dr. Chand: We talked to three cardiologists who knew my lifestyle, and none of them felt it was stress related. They talked about my aging, my narrower arteries, and my diet. I would not eat healthy, but eat everything and anything. They were all pretty clear about it. In fact, Brenda kept asking the cardiologist to "free him." This is what he does—he travels, shouldn't he slow down? Should he not do this? They said, "No, this is good for him." So I really don't have stress in my life. My biggest stress might be running late for a flight, although that rarely happens, because Rachel (administrative assistant and daughter) handles all my travel. Wherever I go, people are very kind to me, very gracious to me. I'm not internalizing anybody else's stress. Brenda is just who Brenda is. She does not create stress for me. She is low drama. Home life is very peaceful. I'm as happy as can be. All three of them said that it was purely physical. So I'm taking care of myself. I was very happy with the doctors' report that there was no heart damage.

Renée: That is so good to hear. So with that, I'd like to ask Brenda a few questions. Brenda, your husband has given you such glowing accolades about how you help him and keep him pretty much stress-free with a happy home life. Can you tell me what is it that you do that can help other pastors' wives and family members help their husbands/spouses to be as emotionally and mentally healthy as possible? What do you do, and what can you say to other spouses?

Brenda: If I might go back to some basics for a moment and look at marriage in general. If you're unhappy as a single person, you're going to be unhappy as a married person. You have to be confident in who you are and whose you are. It took me years to get there. We went through some battles in the very beginning. What I learned was not to expect Sam to be my all and all, to meet all my emotional needs. I'm a person responsible for myself, and if I get bored and have nothing to do while he's away and if I don't have a life of my own, he can't meet that need, no matter what he does. He then can't do what he needs to do because he's so concerned about me. The main thing I've learned over the years is I have to have my own life and not depend on him to meet my emotional needs. I discovered some of these things by first discovering whose I am in Christ. I know that's spiritual language, but you've got to know and be confident that you're a child of God. In seminary when I had to study salvation and spirituality, I learned all these amazing things—that we're God's temple, that we're his daughters, and that won't change. He adopts us and redeems us in a moment when we become a believer. It's remarkable when we realize our position in Christ. That's the spiritual answer.

The practical answer is that we understand and agree on the expectations we have on a practical level. For example, we don't necessarily celebrate our anniversary on our anniversary. We'll have special days due to his travel and we keep the lines of communication open. It's much easier now with technology. It used to be expensive and hard. Now we can communicate at any time. If I'm cracking up because I've heard a joke, I can get on the phone or go online and tell him a joke or tell him a thought that I had. Basically, it goes back to core values. We all have core values. Whether we bring them to the forefront or not, they are there—how we treat people, the respect we have for one another. In our family, you'll never hear demeaning talk or words like "stupid" or "ugly" about one another. So that's a core value of ours we've always had. Mistakes are not the end of the world. We discuss them and we move on. We have a commitment to stay together. Divorce is not an option, pretty much from the beginning. There has never been divorce talk. We work though any issues we might have. Our philosophy is to help others succeed. You probably heard my husband say that many times to leaders, but it's also in the family. Helping each other succeed all the time—that means there is a "no competition" clause in our marriage. We're not competing against each other. We're helping one another succeed.

Renée: I like that... no competition.

Brenda: It helps us express our core values, and it makes us stronger and makes us rich.

Renée: There is such a process of coming into the fullness of who God created us to be. You said it, that it wasn't always that way, even though you had the foundation. It took you some time to realize that Dr. Chand wasn't responsible for your emotional health and well-being. You had to take responsibility.

Brenda: Yes, that's correct.

Renée: That's great advice for other pastors' wives and women in ministry who are married. Nowadays, it appears that we want to give up at the first sign of trouble. Brenda, thank you so much. So Dr. Chand, what's next for you? I know you're working on something.

Dr. Chand: The next project is several things. I have a book coming out in May. My coaching company has created a new program called "Unstuck," meant for churches and corporations where we have a day-long, very highly interactive program that helps companies and churches get unstuck. I am so excited about that. I'm doing a little bit more thinking about what all this means and translates into project. The book is not who I am, but a way of communicating what I'm thinking.

Renée: When it comes to emotional health, to your knowledge, are seminaries and Bible colleges doing more by addressing the emotional and mental well-being of those preparing for the pastorate?

Dr. Chand: More and more of them are doing that, but in different ways, all the way from academic studies to mentoring/discipleship/spiritual formation. It's really all over the map. Degree completion programs have a component in that. It is being addressed—maybe not as aggressively as some would want it to be.

Renée: Would you like to see more of that in the preparation phase for ministry?

Dr. Chand: There is a balance that if you're not careful, you'll soften the program and it will become non-academic. It almost has to be ingrained into every course, rather than a separate program to make you stronger emotionally. I think it can be incorporated in different ways. The challenge is the instructors in the classroom who are older, and especially those who've never pastored. They went from academia to academia and don't have any real-life experience when it comes to leadership. Life experiences are limited for professors, as well. They can get a good book, sit there and read it and teach it, but most academics don't have the real-life experience. And then there are pastors who don't have the academic background teaching at that level. The other thing is that most mega churches today are not being pastored by seminarians. You look at the largest churches in the world, and they may have maybe two years of college under their belt. You're not looking at academics leading our church.

Renée: Am I hearing the old adage that experience is the best teacher?

Dr. Chand: I don't know. It depends on what the experience is. Twenty-five years of experience. It may be one year experience, repeated twenty-five times. It depends on the experience. You might experience dysfunction for twenty-five years. That doesn't mean you have experience.

Renée: So it's the nature and the quality of the experience that shapes the outcome.

Dr. Chand: That's true.

Renée: So how does lack of seminary impact the message? Let's say you've got "good" experience. How does lack of education impact the message?

Dr. Chand: The communicator ends up communicating "user friendly" messages—not trying to be deep theologically, but trying to help you do Tuesday and Thursday, not Greek and Hebrew, but do real life. Most churches supplement with small groups and curriculum-based classes that can do that. You're not going to find theology coming from the pulpit. There are pastors who go through the statement of faith, but that too is once every two years using a theological, but a user friendly format, and not an exegetical theological format.

Renée: To summarize your definition of a healthy soul care provider, you said nine years ago—I gave you the short version when we first started. You said, "A healthy provider is someone who is true to themselves..." which is pretty much the same as what you said then.

Dr. Chand: Yes, I wouldn't change anything

Renée: I guess it's the approach and that times have changed. We have to be more alert and more aware.

Dr. Chand: Yes, people really are more alert.

[END OF CONVERSATION]

Suggested Resources:

Leadership Pain and *Who's Holding My Ladder* by Dr. Sam Chand

Visit *www.samchand.com* for an exhaustive list of other valuable resources.

Considerations?

_____
_____
_____
_____
_____

Confessions?

_____
_____
_____
_____
_____

Convictions?

_____
_____
_____
_____
_____

More Conversations?

_____
_____
_____
_____
_____

MEDITATIONAL SOUL NOTE

For God has not given us a spirit of fear, but of power, and of love and of a sound mind.

—2 Timothy 1:7

CHAPTER 2

MENTAL HEALTH IN THE CHURCH

In Conversation with *Gina Newsome Duncan, M.D.*

D R. DUNCAN EARNED HER B.S. IN CHEMISTRY FROM Hampton University in Hampton, VA, and her M.D. from the University of North Carolina School of Medicine in Chapel Hill, NC. She completed her general psychiatry residency at Harvard at the Massachusetts General Hospital (MGH)/McLean Hospital Adult Psychiatry Residency Program in Boston, MA. In her final year of residency, she served as Chief Resident of Psychotherapy in the MGH outpatient clinic and received the MGH Ann Alonso Award for Psychotherapy. She was also a recipient of the APA/SAMHSA Minority Fellowship and developed a church-based mental health promotion project called Abundant Life Through Applied Resilience (A.L.T.A.R.)™.

Prior to joining Eastover Psychological & Psychiatric Group, Dr. Duncan served as an Assistant Professor of Psychiatry and the Associate Dean for Admissions for the Medical College of Georgia at Georgia Regents University (GRU) in Augusta, GA. While at GRU, she also served as the psychiatrist for Project GREAT (Georgia Recovery-Based Educational Approach to Treatment) and has authored a chapter on Shared Decision-Making in mental health care.

Dr. Duncan is board certified in General Psychiatry. She is a Fellow of the American Psychiatric Association and serves as a blogger on the APA's Healthy Minds website.

Dr. Duncan joined Eastover Psychological & Psychiatric Group in 2015. As a native of North Carolina, she is excited to be closer to family. Dr. Duncan's clinical focus is on the use of medication management and psychotherapy in the treatment of adult Mood and Anxiety disorders, as well as OCD and ADHD. Her other areas of special interest include the intersection of spirituality and psychiatry, disparities in health and achievement that disproportionately affect underserved communities, strength-based approaches to building resilience, and faith and community-based approaches to addressing disparities in mental health.

Married for fifteen years to Dr. Michael B. Duncan II, they are the proud parents of two beautiful daughters, Kendellyn, age 11, and Ava, age 7. They are blessed to call Charlotte, NC, home and to have the love and support of close family and friends.

[BEGINNING OF CONVERSATION]

Renée: As a believer who is a psychiatrist, how does your faith impact your practice?

Dr. Gina: That's a great question. First and foremost, I feel I've been called to this work. I am a believer, and I am a physician who has been trained through medical school and psychiatric residency. I certainly use all of my medical training when I'm working with my patients on determining diagnoses and treatment options. But the greatest impact I have is in my "being" with the patient or in other words, the way I am in the room with the patient. That's a core component of psychiatric training. It's not just about how to prescribe medicine but the psychotherapeutic relationship...who you are with the patient and the importance of bringing your core self into those encounters. So what I bring into every encounter, whether I'm saying it explicitly or not, is that I believe everyone has been created by God and that He has a purpose for everyone's life. Whether they have identified that purpose yet, or are in tune with the calling or not, there is a purpose for everything and for every struggle they're going through. Nothing has happened by chance. So, if that person is in my office at that time, then God has ordained it, and there is something that He is intending to do through me and through them in that encounter. That is how I see my calling.

Dr. Gina Newsome Duncan

Renée: In reading your bio, you developed a church-based mental health promotion project A.L.T.A.R. (Abundant Life

Through Applied Resilience). Tell me more, and is that something you use today with churches and pastors?

Dr. Gina: I am not actively doing the A.L.T.A.R. program at this time, but it continues to be a part of my broader work and my long-term goals. During my residency at Massachusetts General Hospital/McLean Hospital in Boston, I was fortunate to have Dr. Timothy G. Benson as one of my supervisors and mentors. Dr. Benson is also an African American Christian, and graduate of my alma mater, Hampton University. Early in my residency, Dr. Benson and I talked about ways we could do work in the community and specifically in the Black Church. In my fourth year I began the process, with assistance from Dr. Benson, as well as Dr. Valencia E. Miller (who at the time was a Harvard Medical Student) and her husband Carl L. Miller who has a background in social work. I applied for and was awarded a fellowship by the American Psychiatric Association and the Substance Abuse and Mental Health Services Administration to begin the A.L.T.A.R. program. In addition to having experience in the medical and social work fields, the Millers were also members of my church. Our idea for A.L.T.A.R. was to use a focus group format as a way of engaging the community and the church in a discussion around the role of the Black Church in mental health. We would identify barriers, strengths, and ways where there could be better collaboration between the mental health community and faith community. We did not want to do a focus group where we were simply going to go in and solicit ideas from the community for our research. We were very sensitive to the fact that as African Americans, our community has historically been misused by the medical community. The Tuskegee syphilis experiment is one of the most notorious examples. So we wanted to design a program where we would not be going in and just "taking," but giving something, and hopefully getting something out of the dialogue that would help with future research and program development. The program had two components. The first night, we provided psychoeducation and talked about more common forms of mental illness and ways to seek treatment. The second night, Dr. Benson and I did more of a process group. We talked about barriers to mental health treatment that people had experienced or perceived, stigma, and most importantly, ways in which we can enhance our resilience, which is one of the most defining characteristics of the African American community. Our goal was to approach the discussion of mental health from a strengths-based rather than deficit-based perspective. Our idea had been to replicate the focus groups in other churches with the idea of creating a model for churches throughout the country. That is still something I would love to see happen. When I finished residency and joined the faculty of the Medical College of Georgia, I continued to build on the research and have presented on the A.L.T.A.R. model, but in my current private practice, I am not actively engaged in the program. But it was definitely relevant, and I'm drawing on it.

Renée: Yes, it is so relevant. There appears that there is still a stigma in the African American church and the community at large. We hide it, we don't talk about it, we don't address it, and maybe we don't know how to address it. There could even be a type of "stubbornness." You mentioned medication. A diagnosis has been made, but there is such a resistance and refusal to even take the medication. How can we as the church—the pastor, be more responsive to those issues that keep us confined to not really dealing with what I believe is such a prevalent problem today?

Dr. Gina: A great question, and a very big issue in the community. First of all, we must understand that we are not unique in the Black Community when it comes to the stigma surrounding mental illness. It's pretty ubiquitous throughout the world. There are, however, certain communities, countries, and societies where it's dealt with differently.

In the American context, especially the Black American context, one of the reasons there is an extra stigma is that there is already a stigma around being Black in America. I came across this quote when I was doing research related to A.L.T.A.R., and it was the idea that "I'm already black; I don't need to be crazy, too." In other words: "Don't add that additional stigma to me in this society."

In Western societies such as ours, there tends to be an underlying assumption that a person's status is a reflection of their morality—the idea that 'if you're a good person, you shouldn't be struggling.' There is a lot of emphasis on personal responsibility and having it together. If you don't have it together, it's assumed that there is some kind of moral failing on your part. I think the reason we experience stigma as African American Christians when it comes to issues of mental health is because of the general stigma in American society and the fact that we're fighting many battles, just trying to prove our worth to ourselves and to others in this country. So acknowledging that we're not all fine can be a struggle. As far as things that pastors can do, a major area is being mindful of the way their messages are delivered. I listen to a lot of sermons, and I pay attention to the ways in which issues such as anxiety and depression are brought up and discussed. I think a fundamental issue or need is to recognize that psychiatric illnesses are medical conditions, first and foremost. In psychiatry, we think in terms of a bio-psycho-social-spiritual framework; all psychiatric illness has one (if not all four) of those components to it. It is imperative that we recognize that the biological part is real. In our faith communities, we are often unaware of that, nor have we been educated on that. In mental health conditions, the cause is not visible. It's not like having a broken leg where you can see that the leg is broken and a cast is needed. But just because you can't see the neurotransmitter deficiency in the brain doesn't mean it's not actually there. Education is important so that pastors and spiritual leaders are able to more fully embrace the idea that these are medical conditions and should therefore be treated in the same way as other medical conditions. There are now health programs in many of our churches for losing weight, diabetes screenings, blood pressure screenings, etc. The very same thing should apply to our mental health.

One of the things I'm trying to do as I grow in my own practice, is to help patients and others in the community recognize that when someone is presenting with a mental health problem, there may be a biological component that requires medication to address neurochemical imbalances, a psychological component that requires psychotherapy to address the emotional and behavioral aspects, and a spiritual component that requires spiritual interventions such as prayer and spiritual counseling. We need to move away from the notion that it's going to be either/or—either you are going to be spiritually strong and simply "pray it away," or you're going to be spiritually weak and take medication or seek the assistance of a therapist. When it comes to patients of faith who have decided to seek treatment from a psychiatrist or therapist, I think it is equally important that they keep their spirituality in focus and use the opportunity to grow further in their faith by exploring what God may be trying to communicate to them through this struggle and how He may be using the experience to draw them closer to Him.

Renée: It sounds like education is a viable component.

Dr. Gina: Education is tremendous. When we know better, we can do better. So it's important that we not "demonize" our faith community and our pastors. I don't think that they intend to steer people in the wrong way, but in many cases, they just don't have sufficient psychoeducational training. When we in the medical community provide education to our faith community, we have to explain the bio-psycho-social-spiritual dynamic.

Renée: What then should be in place in our churches and our faith community, not only for the parishioners, but for that pastor, chaplain, spiritual counselor, and anyone who cares for the souls of other people? I think we're at "code blue" when we look at the mass shootings and other life-taking events. Usually, it comes out that the shooter has a mental disorder. It's impacting all of us—especially our children and at such an early age. What do we need to do?

Dr. Gina: It starts with a self-examination. We must take a look at ourselves...at our own souls. That's why I like your book title and the term "soul care providers." We start with looking at our own souls and the status of our own emotional and mental health. We have to know the signs and symptoms of common mental health conditions such as anxiety and depression. And then we have to be able to pause and ask the tough questions.

Going back to the education piece, I gave a talk recently at the National Council of Negro Women (NCNW) North Carolina Statewide Convention. I've been trained in mental health, so I know the signs and symptoms of anxiety and depression. But whenever I give presentations like that, many people in the lay community don't know the signs. You have low moods, sleep difficulty, not eating, and other criteria that defines major depression. So it can really go overlooked.

Not knowing what the symptoms are and being able to stop, pause and ask, "How am *I* doing? How is my sleep, how are my eating habits, and my moods? Am I aware of my emotions?" Tuning into ourselves and making sure we have what we need to be emotionally and physically healthy is the equivalent of what they tell you to do in case of an emergency on an airplane: you have to put your own oxygen mask on first before you can assist others. Next, we have to be able to look at our children and take stock of how they are doing on an emotional level. Are there any signs that they may be having a hard time emotionally? Are they withdrawing or acting out? As adults, we create the environment our children live in. We have to look and ask ourselves, "What might I be doing to contribute to the health or unhealth of that environment?" So it all comes back to educating ourselves and to self-examination/self-care as the first step. From there, we can look at the next level of what's going on with the people we love, our immediate circle, then the broader circles of our extended family, our church, our community, etc.

Renée: Let's take that pastor, the church—with all of that, what can be in place? Some churches do have lay counseling, helps ministry, or congregational health programs.

Dr. Gina: I recommend a program called Mental Health First Aid. It trains people in the community to recognize mental health crises and what to do, what are warning signs, and what are signs of an emergency. I think every church should invest in having a few of their parishioners trained in that. However, we can't expect the church to provide total care because when it comes to an individual's health and privacy, there are certain boundaries that have to remain in place and that should not be violated. Every church doesn't necessarily have to have a counseling center, but they can invest in having a few key members trained in mental health first aid, and in putting together a list of community resources that they can provide when someone is in need of mental health services.

They can also plan sermons, programs, and Bible studies to support national mental health awareness initiatives. There are some organizations that provide free online toolkits and resources. These include topics and information for sermons and Bible studies that will address it in a way that acknowledges both the spiritual, biological, and psychological component.

Renée: Do you have a personal counselor or therapist, someone who helps you with your soul care?

Dr. Gina: Yes, I do. I have worked off and on with a therapist since I was in medical school. Having a therapist is encouraged in the mental health field for those of us who are treatment providers, whether you're a psychiatrist, psychologist, or counselor. I recently started seeing a therapist again because providing clinical care can be intense, and I needed to make sure I was paying attention to my own self-care. I need to make sure I can have balance and be as emotionally healthy as I possibly can while I am providing emotional care to my patients.

Renée: Can you share an instance when you might have been suffering emotionally or mentally, and if so, what did you do?

Dr. Gina: Two instances come to mind. I experienced a lot of anxiety in my first couple of years of medical school. It had a lot to do with the pressure of being in medical school and the amount of material I was trying to learn. Having to adapt to that was high pressure, and some of that pressure I was putting on myself. That was when I first starting seeing a therapist. Then in residency, it wasn't so much of test taking anxiety and some other things I experienced in medical school, but trying to juggle the demands of residency with my whole life. We had our first daughter during my intern year of residency and we had moved to Boston, MA, where we had no family or any built-in support. My residency was very competitive and very demanding. Although I enjoyed the work, it was really stressful. My uncle passed away and there were other stressors that we experienced. Having a therapist was really helpful for me because I was also learning how to help provide mental and emotional health care to other people. Day in and day out, I was seeing the struggles and hearing the stories of other people. That's a lot. You start to take that on and start to worry if what is happening to them will happen to you. You want to have empathy for people, but it's a challenge if you start to take everyone home with you. It was important for me to see a therapist then. Even more important, though, was that I grew in my faith during that period of time. Being a member of my church, attending small groups, going to Bible Study, and growing in my personal prayer life and my walk with Jesus was really critical. Those are two instances that come to mind, and my approach to both was to seek help by seeing a therapist, but also to grow in my personal relationship with God.

Renée: You mentioned your uncle passed away. As far as grief is concerned, what happens to our psyche, our mental and emotional stability when we don't properly work through that grief? Sometimes as Christians, we may have a tendency to say, "Just pray about it." We'll say that our loved one is in a better place and is no longer suffering. But I've found that doesn't help emotionally. We call it "incomplete" grief. Loss of a loved one or a loss of anyone or anything significant can be a problem.

Dr. Gina: That's a great question, and I don't know if I have a full answer, except to say that everyone goes through grief in different ways. When I see patients that are experiencing grief, one of the things we talk about is that their process may look different from someone else's, but that's okay. I do get concerned when people appear not to allow themselves the space to fully process the loss they've experienced. What I see in my practice working with patients is that years after the loss, it can become evident when we start to explore current areas of their life that are challenging for them. The grief may then come up and be very fresh, and it becomes apparent that they didn't fully address it. I believe when grief is not fully processed, it can become a depression that can be chronic and long standing.

Renée: As we talk about grief, I just recently looked at a video that was posted on social media about the sudden death of a close relative of a well-known pastor. She was a wife, a mother of four young girls—and she just stopped breathing. It was such a shock, and not only was the family grieving, but the whole church was grieving, so the pastor brought the church together to talk about her death. His daughter, also a well-known spiritual teacher, and his other children were on the stage with him leading the roundtable discussion. They were all visibly shaken while talking about their grief. One of his sons asked his father how he handles all this death because his father also had just lost his brother six months ago. He gave a good answer that showed his leadership as the shepherd being strong for the family and his congregation. His son told his dad how much they love him, admire, and support him, but they were concerned about him. I do not want to be presumptuous and assume something that maybe wasn't the case, but I sensed that maybe they wanted to see more of his grief, his personal pain as a man, an uncle, a brother and not as a pastor. Or maybe that was what I wanted to see.

Dr. Gina: That's why I think the book you're writing is so needed. As far as that pastor was concerned, it could be that he expressed his grief in a more subdued manner because the discussion was done in front of his congregation...I don't know. As a disclaimer, being a psychiatrist, I can't do diagnostic work on someone I haven't met in person. But I imagine for so many of our clergy, there can be a tension between maintaining their role as a source of strength for their congregation and community and expressing their own grief.

I've observed that in my own dad who is a minister. My uncle, who was my father's oldest brother, passed away in 2008. My grandmother passed in 2002 and my grandfather in 2003. Within a span of six years, my dad and his younger brother lost their father, mother, and oldest brother, along with other family members during that time. My father is always called upon to do the eulogies for family members. He dealt with his grief in his own way, but he always pulled it together. Again, what you're doing through this book is really important, because sometimes as soul care providers in whatever field we're in, we don't always know how to allow ourselves to have that space. We don't know how to fully feel, to grieve, or be the vulnerable one when we're used to being the one who's providing the help and the answers.

Renée: Earlier you mentioned you emphasized education when it comes to helping our clergy, our faith communities, to understand emotional and mental illness. You had the fellowship at Mass General, but do you have any plans for a collaborative relationship, a forum, or a program that can be used across the board with the faith community or churches when it comes to education?

Dr. Gina: In the immediate future, no, but in the long term, that is still a goal of mine. In residency, my time was structured differently, and even at the Medical College of Georgia where I was on faculty before moving to Charlotte and going into private practice. There was a certain amount of time that was allocated to research. Being in full-time clinical care over the last few years since moving to Charlotte, my primary focus has been on establishing my practice. But I have done some educational programs in the community and am always open to opportunities to do more. I was recently the keynote speaker for the National Council of Negro Women's NC State Coalition Meeting, and I spoke on the issue of mental health and faith. While I don't have a formal venue for an ongoing program right now, it is something I intend to develop.

Renée: What do we do when the person who is suffering with a mental illness has no insurance and cannot afford the help they need?

Dr. Gina: It's important to be aware of the facilities and services offered through the county or city that provide mental health services on a sliding scale to those with no insurance.

Renée: What do you do when that same person who has a mental illness refuses to acknowledge they need help?

Dr. Gina: If family members are concerned and have been unable to get their loved one to seek help, they could consider making a consultation appointment with a mental health professional to discuss their specific situation and strategies to help their loved one access care. In some cases, if a family member just takes the lead and schedules an appointment, that can lower the barrier sufficiently that their loved one will be willing to come along. Another option is for the family to make the person's primary care physician aware that there are concerns and to request his or her assistance in addressing the matter. Finally, and this is the least ideal, but in more severe cases the family may have to contact the Magistrate's office and get an order for their family member to be taken in for an evaluation, especially if they are a danger to themselves, a danger to others, or so severely impaired that they are unable to care for themselves.

Renée: If that person is suspected of having psychoses and they do get a physical exam, what tests can the doctor perform that might indicate a chemical imbalance or something not wired correctly in the brain?

Dr. Gina: Unfortunately, there are no diagnostic tests for specific psychiatric disorders, but we can perform tests to rule out common physical causes of psychiatric symptoms, for example, anemia or thyroid disorder. We know that there are abnormalities or imbalances in neurotransmitters and other factors that underlie primary psychiatric illnesses, but we are not yet able to reliably measure these in a way that is diagnostic. In a situation where a person is exhibiting a sudden behavior change and there are also signs of a neurological problem such as impaired vision or weakness on one side of the body, then the doctor will likely order an MRI or CT scan, as well as blood work to rule out a neurological disease such as a stroke or tumor.

Renée: Do you have future plans that include a book?

Dr. Gina: Yes. A primary goal of mine is to publish a book that addresses self-esteem, faith, and mental wellness, specifically with an emphasis on African American women. It is a central passion for me. I look forward to your book, which will be a helpful resource!

Renée: Last question—give me your definition of a healthy soul care provider. Include in your definition as a psychiatrist, a woman of faith, what you would say to other soul care providers they must do to be emotionally and mentally healthy or at least be on their way to it.

Dr. Gina: That's a great question for all of us. It is a work in progress. Actually, I met with my therapist earlier today, and one of the things she was talking about is balance. We're always trying to balance the different areas of our life—the different needs and demands.

A healthy soul care provider is someone who is paying attention to the four dimensions of their own health—mental, emotional, physical, and spiritual, and trying as best they can to keep a good balance in each of those areas. It doesn't mean that you won't have times when you get out of balance, because you are busy or you have an illness and may not be able to keep up your exercise as you need to. It is, however, important to keep that goal of balance in mind so that you don't allow your physical health to drop off your radar. Physical health means more than just exercising and eating right; it's also paying attention to and feeling good about your body—the skin that you're in—taking care of yourself in ways that make you feel good. Then there's your emotional health, being in touch with friends and family, and not just giving to others, but also allowing people to pour into you. That is really important.

From a mental health perspective, it means being aware of the signs and symptoms of more common mental illnesses like depression, anxiety, and substance use disorders so that you are aware for yourself and can also educate others. Know what burnout looks like so you can recognize when you're getting overextended, and you can do some things differently. As far as spiritual health, especially for clergy members where most of their time is focusing on the spiritual health of others, make sure to allow people to pour into you spiritually. Finally, recognizing your limitations and knowing where and when to seek help when you need it—It's critical to destigmatize the notion that something is wrong with saying that you need help. To keep everything in balance, it may be that you need to work with a personal trainer for your physical health and to see a therapist or psychiatrist for your mental and emotional wellbeing.

A healthy soul care provider is someone who recognizes their limitations, who does not hold themselves to an expectation that they can take care of everybody else's soul, but that they don't need other people to help in taking care of their soul.

[END OF CONVERSATION]

Considerations?

_____
_____
_____
_____
_____

Confessions?

_____
_____
_____
_____
_____

Convictions?

_____
_____
_____
_____
_____

More Conversations?

_____
_____
_____
_____
_____

"The greatest treasures of wisdom and knowledge are not unearthed during our mountaintop experiences; they are found in the deepest valleys, when we walk hand in hand with the Lord. As much as we would rather avoid the kind of circumstances that take us to a low place, these experiences are essential for our spiritual growth and development. They prepare us for the work to which we are called."

–Kathy R. Green, *Meet Me in the Valley*, Introduction p. xiii

CHAPTER 3

SELF-CARE: HOW SIMPLE CAN IT BE?

In Conversation with *Rita K. Garnto*

RITA K. GARNTO lives in Charlotte, NC, with her husband, daughters, and fur-babies. She recently closed her private massage therapy practice and retired from her 16-year massage therapy career. Her future plans include spending more quality time with family, speaking and spreading the word of how simple self-care can really be, and of course, keeping up with her own simple self-care.

Prior to opening her private massage practice in 2004, Rita said good-bye to her 20-year career in Western healthcare. As a Respiratory Therapist, Rita had the opportunity to work, not only in Canada, her birthplace, but also in Saudi Arabia, and here in the United States. She has cared for patients ranging in age from premature babies to the elderly and everyone in between. During this lengthy career, Rita also had the privilege of being part of the trauma flight team at Carolinas Medical Center in Charlotte, NC. This role allowed Rita to gain the unique experience of caring for critically ill patients during transport flights on helicopters and airplanes. Rita's focus has always been on helping people. Over time, she has come to understand that preventing, or even just lessening, a health crisis is crucial to achieving a better overall quality of life. She saw massage therapy as the way to do this. Thus, she became a licensed massage therapist and began her journey into the world of holistic healthcare. Over time, her mission has evolved into helping ease the pain of aging of her clients through regular massage, self-care education, and awareness. The vast variety of Rita's training and work experience has helped her gain immense insight and wisdom, which has helped shape her into a truly unique self-care practitioner.

"Take care of your body; it is the only one you will ever own." —Rita K. Garnto

---

With a personal journey filled with many challenges including infertility, adoption, family death, and chronic health issues, Rita is no stranger to extreme stress. Based on her own health struggles plus more than thirty-six years of healthcare experience, Rita, as the Simple Self-Care Expert, has developed her own self-care philosophy and the steps to obtain a better quality of health. She has taken the overwhelm out of self-care.

She wants women to understand how powerful just one small self-care change can be and how large of an impact it can have on their future health and well-being. Her mission is to create a global support system for like-minded busy, stressed women that want to make changes to their lives and well-being simply and easily.

[BEGINNING OF CONVERSATION]

Renée: In listening to your story, there are certainly a multitude of life events that qualify you to talk about the holistic nature of self-care. Taking the initiative and responsibility of caring for oneself in the midst of the glaring stressors of life seem overwhelming. Some may say that what you're purporting in your book, *Simple Self-Care Saved Me!* is just not realistic or is even impossible. How do you respond to that?

Self-care is any intentional action you take to care for your mental, emotional, physical, and spiritual health.

Rita: That's the problem, thinking we can't take care of ourselves and do what we need to do. We get very overwhelmed with all the information—we should drink water, eat more vegetables, walk thirty minutes every day, sleep eight hours, and the list goes on. When we see that list of ten, fifteen, twenty things we should do, it gets overwhelming and we stop. So that it doesn't seem impossible, pick one thing. Just pick one simple health care action and make that your focus. For example, thinking that today this *one thing* I'm going to do it for myself—you have to decide what that one thing is going to be. I'm not going to tell you. No one can tell you. It's something that will work for you, and make you feel better, and give you that spiritual boost, a sense of control, and a sense of empowerment. Start with one thing.

Renée: That makes so much simple sense.

Rita: It's crazy because life was supposed to have gotten easier with technology. But we're so inundated with all this information bombarding us and telling us what we need to do, it feels more complicated. We hear that we need to do *this* and then add *that*. So then you decide you're going to walk every day; you're going to drink your water; not eat any sugar; going to eat salad and lean protein for every meal. Then Monday comes along, and you do your walk and your water and maybe you did all those five things. By Wednesday, it might be getting a little tougher: "I've got an early meeting and I can't do my walk, so then why should I do any of it? I talk about this in my book, that we set ourselves up for failure rather than success. It's a mindset change, so after finding that one thing that you're motivated and want to do for yourself, that is your focus for the next week or next two weeks. Every day you say to yourself, "I did it. Yay me." I call it a "yay me moment." It's keeping it simple. I'm guilty though, because I'm the hardest person on myself, but it doesn't need to be so hard. Let's simplify it, and once you've mastered it—that one thing—you become the catalyst. I love the quote, "A journey of a thousand miles starts with one step." You have to start!

Renée: You have to start. I like what you said about the "yay me" moment and how we can be our own worse critic. What I also heard is why not flip that, and rather than being my worse critic, be my best cheerleader, so that my number one cheerleader is me.

Rita: Absolutely. Unfortunately, we've adopted certain patterns over time we use as coping or emotional mechanisms that don't always serve us best. I'm reading a book called the *Five Personality Patterns* by Steven Kessler. Depending on what happened to us in childhood, there are certain ways we now react to stress with such emotion. It's a journey, and not a race. While I didn't realize it, I was doing self-care in my teens, with exercising and journaling, self-medicating the healthy way. I was coping better that way. It was simple.

Four years ago, I renewed my baptism. I was baptized when I was a month old. Five years ago, we found a church that I absolutely love. I found such strength in God and Jesus Christ, and I feel that I have such a purpose to serve. I look back at all the stressors—the awful and difficult challenges I've had have all been for a purpose. I feel like I have to get this message out. It's simple, and we can all do it.

Rita K. Garnto

Renée: Yes, we can...sounds familiar.

Rita: Yes, we can, and with ease.

Renée: We need more ease, because we've got so much dis-ease attacking our bodies, our minds, our spirits, our souls. Tell me about the book, *The Five Personality Patterns*.

Rita: *The Five Personality Patterns* was recommended by a neighbor who is also a massage therapist. I love the language he uses because you aren't "the" pattern, but rather you fall into the pattern. I am not a failure, but that's the pattern of thinking I fall into—that I am, in fact, a failure. Let's stop labeling ourselves. Rather say, this is what I do when I get stressed, but it's not who I am.

Renée: Being a grief recovery specialist, one of the things we look at is patterns of thinking and behavior which causes us to look at family behavior tendencies. If mama, daddy, auntie, or on down the line, had these traits of dealing with stress that aren't healthy, then I need to see if I fall into that same pattern. It doesn't mean that we have to be that way, but we may have those same inclinations.

Rita: Right now, I'm reading the chapter of the pattern I think I fall into. He tells you how to get out of that pattern.

It's all about awareness. If you're aware of something, then you can become motivated and educated to make change happen.

Renée: Sometimes we don't want to visit the past. People may tell us to "just get over it." I understand what people are saying, because sometimes we may tend to wallow in it. But I believe it's necessary to go back, look at certain things to become aware. Education is so vital, and that's part of what you do.

So what was the determining factor that pushed you over the edge to write the book, *Simple Care Saved Me*?

Rita: A good friend of mine kept encouraging me. I've always known I wanted to write a book, but I didn't know what to write about. I was slowly shifting from the massage therapy role to more of the self-care expert with my mission of helping women to get less stressed and healthier. My friend encouraged me to write an eBook. I think too with getting saved and baptized, I felt more and more compelled that I needed to share the struggles I had gone through and the epiphanies I experienced. I have a very unique skill set, with twenty years in the medical field and the sixteen years of massage therapy, and my personality type is that I'm not afraid to share—to stand up and be vulnerable. I used to think it was a curse. I'm not afraid to stand up before a group of people and admit I deal with anxiety. I can say I have been diagnosed with mild anxiety disorder, have been depressed, and had suicidal thoughts. I am willing to say if you feel any of that, it's okay, and let me help you find your way out of that through self-care. Self-care really has saved me. I have brick walls that I run into as a reminder that "Rita, you're not taking care of yourself, so if you're not going to listen to me, I'm going to make you stop."

So back to writing the book—I think it's finding your passion, finding your gift, and doing something with it to make a difference in the world. My good neighbor happens to be an author and has been encouraging me to write the book. She was so gracious and gave me such valuable information on how to begin. It was not easy. With the first draft (they call it the 'poop draft'), she said, "Just write; don't worry about grammar, paragraphs—just get the flow of your ideas down on paper. That made it so easy. I went through it again and fixed it up, and it just flowed by the grace of God. I'm so grateful for this purpose to serve.

Renée: You have such a wealth of experience in the health care field. After that, you opened your private massage therapy business. What was the reason for doing so?

Rita: There were a number of factors. I was approaching forty years old, and the twelve-hour shifts were getting old. I had done that for eighteen years. At the time, I had a good friend who was a massage therapist who I would see regularly for massages. I saw how healing the power of touch was. I really admired that and started asking her questions. It seemed like a viable career change. Honestly, I was becoming so tired of death and dying in the hospital. I've worked in three different countries. I grew up and worked in Canada, and I worked in Saudi Arabia and the United States. I've been on a trauma flight team, worked with adults and premature babies—I've done the gamut of ages, and you get tired. Yes, people do get better and go home, yet you see so many that are dying. In the back of my mind, I thought, *What can I do to help someone so they don't end up in the hospital or maybe be in better shape when they leave? How can I make a difference before people get really sick?* I researched schools for six months and found one in the Charlotte area. It just flowed. I believe when things flow, it was meant to be. I also met my forever husband at massage school, so I can't complain *(laughter)*.

I was working full-time night shift in the pediatric respiratory therapy department. School was part time, one night a week, and then on the weekends. I was able to move my schedule around. It was a lot of work, but it was so worth it.

Renée: I love the whole ambience of the spa and getting the massage. It's all so healing, calm, cleansing. How does massage address the issue of self-care holistically?

Rita: It works on many levels. When you get a good massage, you walk into dimmed lighting, waterfall, music, etc. Because it was my practice, I could take the amount of time I needed. I would do a thorough intake with my clients. When they would come in, we would chat for ten or fifteen minutes before the session. I would book extra time for that. I was able to take the time to find out how they were feeling and where they wanted me to work. By the time they got to the table, they were ready to be quiet because they'd already had the chance to chat. That helped set the stage for the actual touch, the nurturing, healing. It's intimate in a way, not a sexual way, but the way a mother would touch a child where there's feeling of safety and trust. If my clients might fall asleep, they would apologize, and I would hasten to say that was the best compliment they could give me. Because you've let go, you obviously feel very safe and you trust me.

I say a prayer before every massage. I ask that whatever my client may need that it can be given through me and that I would address the tight areas.

So there's the touch, the actual release of tension from the tight muscles; you increase blood flow and the oxygen that goes to the muscles, and it carries away the waste products. You get the softening and loosening of the muscles and decreased pain. It stimulates the parasympathetic nervous system, which is the resting and digesting nervous system. It brings down your heart rate, lowers blood pressure, etc. Physiologically, you've got lower blood pressure, lower heart and respiratory rate; your digestive system is actually allowed to start working. Have you ever wondered why your stomach gurgles when you're on the massage table, or you have to go to the bathroom after a massage? It's because your parasympathetic nervous system has kicked in and your digestive track has been allowed to do its thing. Blood sugar will normalize because you're not stressed. You've activated the opposite nervous system as you would when you're stressed.

When your body is allowed to relax and you feel comfortable and safe, the mind is able to let go. There is also endorphin release, which makes you feel comforted and safe. I put heat packs on my clients back when they first start the massage. They feel very cocooned.

Renée: It's interesting as you were describing the whole scenario, I was feeling so calm as if I was actually there at the spa getting a massage. That speaks to the mind.

Correlate the physiological as you just described to someone who is dealing with an emotional or mental disorder. How does that massage help them? Not that it will automatically cure it, but what does it do for the those suffering mentally?

Rita: It depends on if it's more anxiety related. As the client gets the massage, it's activating the resting digesting nervous system to allow the adrenaline and cortisone levels to come down, and not on hyper stressed out mode. They are able to relax and hopefully slow down the thoughts in your head. When I get overwhelmed, I start thinking what I have to do in rapid succession, but then I stop and take a deep breath and slow down to activate that nervous system. That helps to clear my head. Exercise does the same thing, which is good too.

Lots of studies have come out now that show how massage is so helpful for anxiety and depression. It's also reassurance that the client has somebody listening to them, that they care and are being nurtured. The physiological is where the resting digesting nervous system is being activated and all the other physiological things that I previously described, so it's all working together.

Studies have shown that with consecutive massages, the benefits exponentially happen. If your budget allows you to go regularly, the benefits will be greater over time. Even if you can't go as often such as weekly or every two weeks, I wonder if your body has the memory of your last massage and says, "Here I am again in the massage office and I get to relax." The power of the mind already lowers the stress, tension, and anxiety level before you get on the table.

Renée: The brain is so complex. Being a health practitioner with a medical background that understands the mechanics of the body, talk about how chemicals released in the brain affect your thinking.

Rita: Take away the complicated chemicals, think about what we tell ourselves, the thoughts we have. You do something and you say, "I'm such an idiot." You just called yourself an idiot! Well, you're not an idiot, but you're criticizing yourself. So I've learned to laugh at myself more. I roll my eyes at myself and then say, "I can't believe I just did that," and laugh, rather than saying, "you're so stupid, Rita."

The power of the messages that we tell ourselves—you look in the mirror and tell yourself, "Oh my gosh, I'm so fat, so ugly, so old."

So I say to myself, "Look at me, I'm 55. Don't I look great, and just went for my walk. Yay me." Tell yourself you're beautiful. The power of the mind plays such a large role.

Years ago when I was eighteen, my best friend from high school sent me a birthday card that read, "Imagine the woman you want to be, now start acting like her and eventually you'll be her." That stuck with me!

We tell our kids, if you can't say anything nice, don't say anything at all! And then we turn around and tell ourselves, "I'm such a loser. I'm such a terrible mom."

Renée: You also mentioned breathing. In one of your former lives, you were skilled as a Respiratory Therapist. How does breathing affect our emotional and mental well-being?

Rita: We look for complicated things, but just taking three deep breaths is one of the simplest ways to activate that parasympathetic nervous system. When I'm feeling overwhelmed and kind of *crazy* (probably a bad choice of words) like a hamster on a wheel, I'll put my feet on the floor. It's signaling to my body that I'm grounding—I'm stopping for a moment. I'll take a deep breath and fill up my lungs, pause, and slowly exhale. It pulls you into the moment rather than thinking about your "to do" list. We forget to be in the moment. Deep breathing helps us stop, pause, and just be. It's that awareness thing again - being aware that I'm in my body, aware of where my shoulders are...oh they're up by my ears; oh better let those relax...just checking in.

Until you just asked me about breathing and being a respiratory therapist, I didn't think of putting the two together, and now I'm talking about deep breathing and activating the parasympathetic nervous system.

Renée: Connecting the dots!

Rita: Thank you, Renée

Renée: I like what you said about just checking in and being. We're so programmed to *do* that we forget to simply *be*. Just *be* in the moment and check in with yourself periodically.

Rita: That's a reminder for me. In the last few days, I haven't been doing that. I've been feeling stressed. I'm an ambitious woman, and I've got lots of things I want to do. I stop and think, *my kids are safe and fed, everybody's okay, and there's no danger.*

Why can't I stop and take three deep breaths? If I don't answer that email or contact that person, why not stop and fill our emotional bank? Have a "yay me" moment and then carry on!

Renée: Prior to opening your private massage practice in 2004, you said goodbye to your twenty-year career in "Western health care." Why the emphasis on western health care, and did your exit lead to a different mindset about holistic health care?

Rita: Western health care is relatively new, just a few hundred years old. Our system is pharmaceutically driven where we treat the symptoms, not the cause. It's a money-making machine. Now there have been wonderful and amazing advancements with trauma and burn victims, saving premature babies, organ transplant—saving people. We couldn't do without it. With the acute "life on the line" emergencies, we've made great advancements. Where we fall short in the Western health care system is with our maintaining a quality of health. So I come in to the doctor's office and I'm stressed, my blood pressure is up. I take a pill to bring my blood pressure down, but it artificially brings it down. The fact that my blood pressure is up may be because of my stress level, or I've not been taking care of myself. That needs to be much more addressed. I'm seeing a shift now where it's more about prevention. So when I talk about western health care, I think about taking a pill to treat the symptoms, for example, as in back pain. Here's this pain pill to make the pain go away, but there's still a problem. That's where massage therapy comes in. I could help with the problem—with the muscle imbalance, or refer you to a chiropractor that will deal with the skeletal imbalance. We could work as a team together. Perhaps I could refer you to an acupuncturist or physical therapist, depending on what I felt you'd benefit most from. That is really getting to the root of the problem, not just treating the symptoms.

Does that make sense?

Renée: Yes, indeed. Now I'm going to shift to an Eastern approach to self-care. You take a Taekwondo class. What motivated you to do that?

Rita: We became a new family in January 2009 with my eighteen-month-old and almost four-year-old daughters, and heard about this new school that taught Taekwondo. We thought it would be really good for our oldest daughter who had a difficult first life before we became family. There were self-confidence issues and there had been some abuse. We wanted to give her the best chance to arm herself and work through that. At the recommendation of our next-door neighbor, we went to check out the school. However, we went to the wrong one.

The reason I bring that up is that I've always been active and played sports. After my back and knee surgery, I had to modify my active lifestyle. If I can't go running, then I'll walk. It's all about modification. So I asked the instructor, do you think I can do this? After I explained my knee and back problems, I was told no, that it would be too much for me. "It's a lot of kicking and wouldn't be good for you." So we left that school without signing up. After talking with our neighbor, we realized we had gone to the wrong school.

So when we went to the correct school and asked the same question, I was told, "Of course you can do this! Just do what you can; modify where you have to, and you can still partake." That just made complete sense. Again, simple! If you can't do something, just adapt. I was in my forties at the time. I started off with the little kids' classes. That was good for me because I had no experience, and I could start off with the little kids. My girls saw me doing it, and that encouraged them to see they could follow instructions—that they could do it too! I was their role model, and it was also great mom and daughter time. Over the years, I've had to take some time off with knee and back issues and also neck surgery, but I keep going back because it's about discipline and doing what you can do. I can't do what the eighteen-year-old boys and young men can do, but I do my best. I'm now working on my third degree black belt. As I achieve that, I'm not compared to anyone else—I'm compared to what I can do, and then I have to pass the physical fitness tests and other tests. It's a bit of a challenge. I'm going to do this! So I challenge myself. Why can't I do this? Who says at the age of fifty-five I can't do this? It becomes another "yay me" moment. It's taken me nine years, and for someone else, it may not have taken them as long. But it's not about them. It's about empowering myself.

Renée: So that brings me to the litany of life events in your personal journey—the challenges of infertility, adoption, family deaths of close loved ones, chronic health issues. Each event is extremely emotionally charged and enough to wreak havoc in your mental equilibrium. I'm assuming that the infertility led to adoption. With this assumption, talk about the unique attention that you and your husband receive as a Caucasian couple with two bi-racial daughters. How do you care for your soul and the souls of your daughters? Describe a simple self-care approach that you employ.

Rita: My husband and I got married when I was forty years old and got pregnant right away. Over the next few years, I had four miscarriages. During that time, we did some infertility treatments. It's interesting that my husband always felt even as a teenager that he would be an adoptive father, which I thought was quite unusual for a young man. It was always a topic of conversation, because I was already forty. I had this hope that we would have our own child. After a couple of miscarriages, we started on the adoption pathway because we knew it would take a little while.

With private adoption in the United States, typically you'd adopt a newborn baby. When we started off on this journey, I wanted to have children that looked like me. We wanted a blond, blue eyed girl. I have a friend who is African American, and we would often get together for coffee and talk. I don't know when it happened, but it dawned on me, I just want to be a mom. Skin color and ethnicity just didn't matter to me. I grew up in Canada and was first-generation Canadian and grew up in such a diverse community. I'd ask my friends, "What nationality are you?" We'd say we were German, Ukrainian, East Indian, Italian; Scottish—we never said we were Canadian, but many of us were first-generation, and we had the cultures of our parents' country.

We were in the running for another baby, but they decided on another couple. The way we became a family with our daughters was so unusual. As time went on in our adoption journey, I started to visualize this little mocha-colored child—this little girl with beautiful mocha-colored skin and big brown eyes. (I believe very much in creative visualization.) So one day, we got the phone call from our adoption consultant. She asked if we were sitting down because they had this unusual situation. They had two little girls who are sisters. Twelve days later, we were parents! That's another story in itself. That's another book!

The first time I went to my oldest daughter's school, one of the kids said, "That's your Mom???" And I said proudly, "Oh yes, I am! It has really helped to open up cross-cultural and ethnic boundaries.

When we first got the girls, my oldest daughter had a lot of beautiful curly hair. And we just didn't know how to take care of it. Her birth mother showed me how to do twists and braids, and I got pretty good with it. But my husband started asking all the African American women he worked with, "How do I take care of my daughter's hair?" Now, my husband used to be very private and did not open up very much. All of sudden, he was ordering all these different products that his co-workers told him to use on our daughter's hair. I thought it was so cool, this white man, a computer engineer who was so hyper-focused on conquering her hair. He found her hair fascinating. He said he was going to conquer this hair! I became so aware of these beautiful hairstyles, and I would say that my daughter's hair is like your hair. What do you use? It opened doors and communication and relationships that normally wouldn't have happened. I am so blessed and so proud. Especially living in the South, we tell the girls, you may run into some issues, but skin color doesn't matter, it's who you are inside because God made you this way. From day one, we talked about the fact they're adopted. They look more like my husband with brown hair and brown eyes. It's our norm, and I'm humored because when we're out and about, I may say to the girls, "I wonder where's your dad?" And people are expecting this black guy to walk up so when my husband appears, they are perplexed. To see the look on people's faces, we think it's funny watching them as they try to figure it out. I just smile at them. It's become more and more common—races and ethnicities blending, which is fabulous.

So you asked me to describe a simple self-care approach that I employ. Not making it complicated. This is who we are as a family. If you don't like it, don't hang out with us. This is the way it is.

Renée: The operative word—SIMPLE, it's not complicated!

Rita: If you have a question, ask. We share. We have several friends who have adopted from Asia, and it's probably similar for them, as well. It just opens up avenues of communication and support and love. Our world needs so much more of that.

Renée: It's so needful. In whatever way we do that, the fact that it's done is so immense. It goes a long way, longer than we think.

Rita: One of the biggest problems with this world is fear—fear of the unknown, fear of something different than me. The more we can talk and have open communication about our difference, it opens the door for greater understanding of our belief systems, culture, our differences. It opens the way for more peace and more love.

Renée: What's the song … "What the world needs now is love, sweet love; it's the only thing that there's just too little of."

Rita: Absolutely, now more than ever.

Renée: There's another quote from your book that resonates, "When you're mired in your muck, to get unstuck do one new thing, just change one little thing." You also emphasized that "self-care is about self-preservation and not self-indulgence. I think we need to change our mindset; those in the soul care world…doctors, care givers of children, an aging parent, pastors, etc. We women especially tend to think that we're being selfish, self-indulging, and not self-preserving.

Rita: I think that we as women typically feel guilty for doing things for ourselves. But if your cup is empty, you can't do that. For example, if I wake up with a headache and don't do any simple self-care (which is as easy as warming up and using my organic flaxseed neck wrap), I end up being crabby to my girls. It has a ripple effect. If our house is full of very little patience, lots of frustration, and irritability, I'm setting my girls up to have a bad day. So then they talk to their friends, and snap at them, and hurt their feelings, and so on. The ripple effect—my empty cup has now affected many more people than just my daughters and myself. So if I can keep my cup full and take care of and love myself, then I'll do a much better job of taking care of others who will, in turn, take better care of others.

Renée: You mentioned pastors. I think one of the challenges with our pastors is needing that sabbatical, needing that retreat and not taking it fully.

Rita: I agree. Our pastor was given a grant to take off three months with her family to renew her spirit and to simply be recharged. She's in charge of the church and taking care of us. However, giving the time needed for pastors takes planning and forethought. It takes the congregation to stand behind their leader and step up while the pastor is gone. While she was away, we had a guest pastor; we had someone doing pastoral care. There were four or five people filling her role while she was gone. Others of us took turns doing something, because it takes a village. As I said, it needs to be intentional and planned, and not just to say that they need to take a vacation. Most importantly, their time away should be honored. Our pastor is completely unplugged from social media, she's not receiving texts/calls but completely stepped away. She is allowed to have that opportunity to disconnect so she can hear the whispers from God and be recharged and renewed when she comes back. It takes planning, intention, and support. You can't care for people 24/7 without giving to yourself.

My mom died when she was seventy-five from a massive heart attack. She did a little bit of self-care, but she kept a lot of stuff inside. The last few years before she passed away were very stressful. I believe stress did her in. She didn't ask for help. She didn't allow herself to be supported and was not intentional in taking time away. She ended up dying, which was the ultimate sacrifice.

Renée: We must take care of self. It's the only one we have. I close our conversation with a quote from your book:

"Simple self-care is any intentional self-care action that is easy, not rocket-science nor complex, and effortlessly slides into your day."

How simple can that be?

[END OF CONVERSATION]

Suggested Resources:

Simple Self-Care Saved Me! Superpowers Included, by Rita K. Garnto, http://simpleselfcare.net

Considerations?

_____
_____
_____
_____
_____
_____

Confessions?

_____
_____
_____
_____
_____

Convictions?

_____
_____
_____
_____
_____

More Conversations?

_____
_____
_____
_____
_____

"A healthy soul care provider is someone who does not take him or herself too seriously but takes God very seriously."

—the late Dr. Phillip M. Davis, quote from thesis, *The Biblical Counselor: A Healthy Profile of the Soul Care Provider in the 21st Century Church,* by Renée Hill Carter

CHAPTER 4

YOUR EMOTIONAL HEALTH—IT'S ALL UP TO YOU!

In Conversation with *Dr. Mark Croston*

D R. MARK ANDREW CROSTON, SR. was born in Philadelphia, Pennsylvania. He is the eighth of nine children born to the late Reverend Nathaniel Moses and Isabella Croston, Sr.

Dr. Croston came to know the Lord at an early age, and was baptized at the Liberty Baptist Church of Philadelphia.

He earned a Bachelor of Science degree in Engineering from the University of Pennsylvania. He received a Master of Divinity Degree with a concentration in Pastoral Care and Counseling from The Southern Baptist Theological Seminary in Louisville, Kentucky. Reverend Croston completed his studies and earned the Doctor of Ministry degree, concentrating in Christian Education, at Virginia Union University,

Richmond, Virginia. Formerly, Dr. Croston was employed by the IBM Corporation as a systems engineer.

Three years after the death of his first wife, Dr. Croston married his current wife, Brenda. This blended family has four children: Candace, Juliette, Mark, Jr., and Antonio.

Dr. Croston is the author or contributor to several books including *Big Results: Sunday School and Black Church Life; Removing the Stain of Racism from the SBC; The Chosen Path, Seeds of Hope: Liberia and Virginia Baptists; From My Heart to Yours* and *Worship: How to Say to God I Love You*. His doctoral dissertation is titled *Intentional Christian Education in a Rural-Urban African American Church and Community*. He is a sought after Conference Presenter and Revival Preacher. As a man on a mission Dr. Croston has been privileged to do quite a bit of domestic and international travel. As a man on mission he has traveled in Antigua, Aruba, Bahamas, Barbados, Canada, Chile, Egypt, England, Germany, Cayman Islands, Greece, Haiti, Holland, Israel, Italy, Jamaica, Kenya, Martinique, Mexico, Panama, Puerto Rico, St. Croix, St. John, St. Kitts, St. Lucia, St. Maarten, St. Martin, St. Thomas, Saudi Arabia, Senegal, South Africa, Switzerland, and Trinidad.

At the end of 2013, after twenty-six years of successful pastoral ministry at East End Baptist Church, Suffolk, Virginia, Dr. Croston, in response to the call of God, transitioned to serve as National Director of Black and Western Church Partnerships at LifeWay Christian Resources in Nashville, Tennessee. He has also served as General Editor and Writer for the YOU Urban Bible Study Curriculum, Teaching Pastor of Christ Fellowship, Miami, Florida, and Executive Pastor of Mount Gilead Baptist Church, Nashville, Tennessee. Additionally, Dr. Croston has been conferred the title of Pastor Emeritus of East End Baptist Church, Suffolk, Virginia.

In the denomination, Dr. Croston has served as President of the Baptist General Association of Virginia; President of the

Virginia Baptist State Convention; President and Treasurer of the National African American Fellowship of the Southern Baptist Convention; Guest Lecturer for The Southern Baptist Theological Seminary; Member of the African American Advisory Committee for the SBC Executive Committee; Member of the Nominating Committee for the Southern Baptist Convention; President of the African American Fellowship SBC of Virginia; Member of the National Baptist Convention, USA, Inc; Financial Secretary, Sharon Baptist Association; and Moderator of the Portsmouth Baptist Association. He has also served as Chairman for African American Taskforces for NAMB, IMB, and LifeWay.

His involvement in the community has included his work as Chairman of the Suffolk City School Board; Member of Civic Leadership of Hampton Roads; Chairman, Suffolk City-wide MLK Day Celebration Committee; President, Suffolk Civic Forum; Vice Chairman of the Board of the Nansemond Credit Union; Board Member, Paul D. Camp Community College; and President, Suffolk Interdenominational Ministerial Alliance.

[BEGINNING OF CONVERSATION]

Renée: What does it take to be emotionally healthy as a pastor and who is responsible?

Dr. Croston: It's up to that pastor to think about what they need and to keep themselves healthy. Some do that better than others. The times and things you go through will make a difference in what's required in those particular areas.

Someone said to me that this must be your busy time. No, all the year is busy—it's just busy in different ways. Each person has to take their own path. I don't know that there is one way for everybody. Our makeups are different. Sometimes, we try to push everybody into one way of doing things. "Everybody needs to do this." Well, I'm not sure everybody needs to do all of those things.

Today, a number of guys (pastors) said they've been taking sabbaticals—one month, two months, or three months. That can be great, but I don't think that's the path for everybody. That's the key; each person needs to find their path and what works for them.

The older preachers years ago used to always take a month of vacation during the summertime. They never called that a sabbatical. Today, it's called sabbatical. They called it vacation, but it's basically the same thing.

Long respites would not work for me. For me, a month off would drive me crazy.

Renée: Why is that?

Dr. Mark Croston

Dr. Croston: There is always something to do. There's a part of me that is always excited about the ministry and wants to do it. If you're passionate and want to do it, that's a great thing. But you still have to make sure you're revived and rested enough. I've done different lengths of vacation over the years.

When I started out right from seminary into the ministry, they gave me two weeks of vacation time in my package. Later after I'd been there for about ten years, I went to the personnel committee and said that I needed a month of vacation every year. They asked me why, and then told me I could take off any time I wanted. My church was very good about that; they were not sticklers about how much time or when. Some churches are, but my church was not.

I said, "I know, but I need it for 'bragging rights.'" They asked, "What do you mean?" When I go to these meetings with preachers, somebody will ask, "How much vacation time do you get?" I don't want to say I only get two weeks; I want to be able to say I get a month off. Even though in a real sense, it didn't matter to them how much time I took off because they knew I was focused, that I was a worker. When you have that reputation of being a worker and focused, the amount of time you take off is less important to your congregation. I know some pastors who have reputations of playing golf or fishing all the time and people are wondering where they are; they didn't come to the office. They become overly concerned about your time. But if you have a reputation of being honest, being on the task, I think they lighten up and stop worrying about that. That's the kind of relationship we had, and I could take off when I wanted to.

So I tried different lengths of time off to determine for my-self what really felt best—a week off, a few days off during the week, a weekend off, five days off, or two weeks. For me, a seven or eight day cruise was my optimum vacation time. Something about being on the water was extremely restful for me and that time frame was enough for me to feel relaxed but not bored. I tried ten-day cruises and tried a little shorter cruise, but realized my favorite vacation is a cruise, and the seven to eight days is my optimum length to feel rested, reenergized, and revived.

The good thing is you can't get phone calls, texts, or emails (unless you buy computer time). It helps you to just cut off and leave the crises and emergencies to somebody else.

Renée: It sounds like you've just described what an emotionally healthy person is once they determine for themselves what works and are not looking at somebody else.

When you go to pastors' gatherings and conferences, you mentioned "bragging rights" about time off. That takes me to another point that might lend itself to an unhealthy trait. Is there sometimes a sense of competition or having to make yourself look as good as the next one? How prevalent do you think that is?

Dr. Croston: That depends on the individual person; some are, and others aren't. At my first pastorate, the pastor before me was at the church during my first twenty years. He had been there forty-three years as pastor before I got there. He retired at seventy-eight, and didn't die until he was ninety-eight. We were together for twenty years after he retired. When I got to our city, I was a young upstart pastor in town; I wanted to talk about the new trends and new things I was trying to do at our church. My pastor was from a whole different generation and he said, "I wouldn't do that...I wouldn't tell the other preachers what you're doing because they might want to copy it." I told him that's exactly what I want them to do because if they start doing this, it will make it easier for me to make changes in our church if our church sees others making changes too.

We're in this thing together. I tell my guys there are more sinners out there that can fill all our churches and have a lot of sinners left over. There's no reason to feel I'm in competition, because our supply is endless. If you think that way, why should we be in competition with anybody else? There are too many fish in the ocean.

Some guys may feel the pressure to conform. Preachers are human first. For some, there is this pressure to conform, and be like everybody else, or be beyond everybody else. For me, I just wanted to push my church along, and I knew I wanted to bring other pastors along in the city. Traditional churches don't like to feel too far out of step with everybody else. Some handle the pressure better than others.

Renée: It sounds like you were a wise young man and pastor who respected and was willing to listen to those older than you with more experience. You wanted to show him the wisdom in what you were doing. Did he understand and accept you at first?

Dr. Croston: For most of those years, we had a great relationship. Naturally, he and I were cut from two totally different cloths. He was very old school—very high church. Even though he grew up in a Baptist church, he was trained in a Presbyterian seminary. He bought all of the elements of Presbyterian life to our church. It took me a little while to see that it was a Presbyterian church with a Baptist name on it. Once I realized what I was working with, it became easier to manage and I understood what it is. Though I am a little more demonstrative than the pastor who came before me, I told the church that this is who I am and I can't be anybody else but me. However, I never changed the polity of the church because it was working. He had some angst in the beginning, like how I presented myself in worship, which was a bit more active than what he was used to.

About two years after I arrived, this older pastor got an opportunity to preach at his home church in another city. When he was a young man, that church was "the" church—everybody went there. It was the largest church in town, and everything was great. But when he went back to preach in his retirement years, what he found was a cavernous auditorium with a few gray-haired people sitting around. They had just called a young man to pastor. It broke his heart. He came back a changed man. He reflected how he had poured his life into this church, and he didn't want what happened at that church happen to us. "Whatever you have to do, you just do it. You have my entire support." From that day on, we had a tremendous relationship as colleagues, sometimes like father and son, until the day he died eighteen years later.

Pastors are people; whether you're working in the ministry, as a lawyer, doctor, or some other profession, you still have to carve out times and scenarios in your life that will help refresh you—maybe even more so in helping ministries and helping professions. Even though they tell you not to take the work home with you, the truth is you can't do this work and not take some of it home.

Renée: And be true to the call?

Dr. Croston: Yes!

CARE FATIGUE

Dr. Croston: When Hurricane Katrina hit New Orleans, many people left, but many pastors stayed. Most of the pastors who stayed or many who came back, eventually left again because of care fatigue. When you're caring for people in normal people crisis, that's one level of care fatigue, but where everybody around you is in crisis mode with nowhere to live, no money, that's a different intensity. With such a catastrophe as Katrina, it takes that care fatigue to a whole new level. So many of the pastors that were in New Orleans changed because of that fatigue over the years of trying to care for people in the midst of that entire crisis. I don't know if we ever think about that. I'm sure somebody has a statistic of how many are still there and how many are gone.

Renée: In today's culture, it seems we're in a perpetual crisis mode with such an escalation of tragedies. Most people probably think that surely the church can help us with this devastation, how we're feeling, give us some hope. How do the pastor and the church balance that?

Dr. Croston: I don't think the church knows it unless the pastor brings it up. Does the pastor even see it?

PERSONAL GRIEF

My first wife died of breast cancer in 2008. She had her first battle in 1998. She passed just before Thanksgiving in 2008. Right after she passed, we had three other members in the church who died and another close family member in the same city (not the same church) who died. Now, I'm going through my own grieving, and members certainly appreciated it, but in their mind after my wife's funeral, they're back to business as usual.

Two weeks after my wife's death, I did two funerals and attended one at another church all before Christmas. Then the fourth death occurred, but I just couldn't handle another funeral. Even though I was at the funeral, I had to assign the eulogy to another minister at the church. The family, of course, was very upset with me that I did not do my pastoral duty of doing the eulogy, although I explained where I was emotionally with still grieving my wife's death.

About a year after my wife's death during the Pastor's Appreciation, I wrote an article in our church newsletter titled, "Who Cares for the Pastor." I took some time in the article of reflecting what the past year was like for me with my struggles. In a gentle way, I reminded the congregation that at times, it's your job to care for the caregiver. Some people liked the article, and some people didn't like it. That was neither here nor there.

Renée: That's exactly what we're talking about. I think it is so important that the church knows how to deal with grief, especially after the funeral. As you said, people revert back. Just as you've alluded, you were still grieving your wife, yet the church expected you to carry on as normal. This reminds me of when Bishop Davis died, it was important that the congregation knew how to deal with their grief and the grief of others.

How can we educate the church and people in general to understand the dynamics of grief? As a certified grief recovery specialist, I have come to appreciate the aftermath of the death of a loved one.

Dr. Croston: There is similarity between Phil's (Bishop Phillip M. Davis)death and my wife's death. In his death, there was no advanced notice. In my wife's death, even though they knew (the church) about the onset of her cancer in 1998, she became more private and many didn't know it had returned. I felt we should have prepared others, especially our children. She wasn't ready to talk about it or reveal it to anybody because she felt it would have appeared as a lack of faith. She believed that God would heal her, even though the doctors told her otherwise. I recognized I was going to be the one here, and I needed to have that conversation to prepare them.

After she passed, I further prepared them that the church is grieving, and I think they will go crazy for a little while, and they did. I don't know a way for that not to happen. They went crazy for a little while, but eventually they came back to themselves. Sometimes in the craziness, there is damage that you can't fix, and I think that happened in a few people's lives.

Renée: How did you personally deal with your grief after you wife's death? Were there support systems in the church that did allow you your time of mourning and grief?

Dr. Croston: I preached sermons that were helpful for me. All my sermons were for me; other people got to listen in to what the pastor needed to preach to himself. They probably didn't hear it that way, but I knew what I was thinking in this whole process. One thing I know about people, all have basically the same issues, no matter what culture, country, language, tribe, male or female, or ethnicity. If I needed some of those healing messages and hope, they needed it too. Although I'm preaching it for me, they're hearing for themselves.

Renée: Did you take your respites?

Dr. Croston: I took small periods of rest at different intervals, a week here or a few days. Some pastors said that I should have taken three or six months off. Well, if that works for you, okay, but not for me. Again, people need what they need and figure out what does or doesn't work for themselves.

THE TRUST FACTOR AND LONELINESS IN LEADERSHIP

Renée: I've heard that pastors sometimes don't trust and that pastoring is a lonely deal. They don't have a lot of friends. There's sometimes a connection between not having a lot of friends that is supposedly because they don't trust. What's your take on that?

Dr. Croston: Lonely and trust are two different issues.

The loneliness of Leadership is not unique to the pastor. I tell pastors, especially younger pastors, "Eagles soar alone, and vultures fly in packs." We see an eagle as such a great symbol of leadership.

Leaders are often alone. They're willing to go places other people won't go, do things other people won't do. Often, it takes seasons of reflection, and I can't always do that in a crowd. If I'm going to be a leader, I've got to be willing to separate myself from those who will not go with me. If I always feel like I've got to have my boys, maybe there's some portion of that that won't let me be the best leader I could be.

Leadership, regardless of the profession, is often a lonely endeavor.

But I don't think it's necessarily lonely because of the trust issue. The most godly people I know that stand in leadership as pastors don't have trust issues, even though life may seem lonely at times. It's not a trust issue, but it's because you won't find people who are willing to go this way. The Bible says that broad is the way that leads to destruction, and there are plenty of people on that road. But straight is the gate and narrow is the way that leads to everlasting life, and you only see a fellow traveler every now and then. So if you're running with too many people, maybe you're not running in the right direction, because most people don't want to make the sacrifice Jesus is calling for. I sent out a tweet that maybe the reason for so much selfishness in our politics, businesses, and our religious circles is that preachers have stopped preaching what Jesus said, to deny himself, take up his cross, and follow me.

We want a God of plenty and pleasure, but that is not the God of the Bible, that's the God of a few verses.

I was reading an article written by Jessie Campbell in *Explore the Bible* curriculum about Jeremiah 29:11 which is often misinterpreted. But verse 10 talks about the length of their suffering being seventy years, but we use it to talk about the fact that God is leading us to this place of prosperity and hope. But it is talking about the fact that He will be good to us and preserve us, even though we're going through seventy years of suffering.

Renée: In conclusion, Dr. Croston, what is your definition of a healthy soul care provider in today's church?

Dr. Croston: Let me put it this way—pastors should:

- Be in touch with God and themselves.
- Recognize their own humanity.
- Take the opportunity to receive the care that they need for themselves, and give themselves care as they give care to others.

[END OF CONVERSATION]

Considerations?

_____

_____

_____

_____

_____

Confessions?

_____

_____

_____

_____

_____

Convictions?

_____

_____

_____

_____

_____

More Conversations?

_____

_____

_____

_____

_____

Be still, and know that I am God:
I will be exalted among the nations,
I will be exalted in the earth!

—Psalm 46:10

"People in a hurry never have time for recovery. Their minds have little time to meditate and pray so that problems can be put in perspective. In short, people in our age are showing signs of physiological disintegration because we are living at a pace that is too fast for our bodies."

—Archibald Hart

CHAPTER 5

WHEN SHE'S OUT FRONT

In Conversation with *Mr. Gilbert and Rev. Dr. Barbara L. Peacock*

M R. GILBERT PEACOCK, business owner of Freedom Financial Advantage, is a Licensed Financial Professional working with a diverse client base of business owners and many other trade and professional people. Gilbert has learned about the stock market as an individual investor since 1975. He conducts training sessions with groups and individuals to educate and develop financial plans and insurance strategies.

His education includes General Management Studies at Queens University, Charlotte, NC and a BS Degree, Business Marketing, Florida A&M University, Tallahassee, FL.

Dr. Barbara Peacock is passionate about teaching, ministering, praying, and spiritual direction. She is the founder of United Praying Women of Barbara L. Peacock Ministries

(BLP Ministries). An experienced preacher, teacher, and minister of discipleship and prayer, Barbara trains in spiritual direction/coaching and soul care for ministry leaders. Dr. Peacock has a God-given call and desire to serve as spiritual coach for individuals and groups. The goal is for them to experience a deeper relationship with God that can lift their spirits, and thus propel them to accomplishing all that God has called them to be and do. She is the author of *Psalm 119 Journal* and leading author for *C.A.L.L.E.D. to Teach.*

In her journey to assist others in experiencing a more intimate relationship with God, she also serves as a speaker with the Exponential Group, an organization that utilizes a proven godly fundraising model to create a tailored solution for faith-based non-profit organizations, started by well-known speaker and author of *The Prayer of Jabez,* Dr. Bruce Wilkinson. Dr. Peacock's preaching and teaching opportunities have included:

- Speaker at Women's Luncheon hosted by Dr. Suzan Johnson Cook at the Hampton Ministers Conference
- Spoke in Isiolo, Kenya
- Women's Services and Conferences and Prayer conferences
- C.A.L.L.E.D. to Teach trainings

Barbara served on staff for fourteen years as Minister of Discipleship and Prayer at The Park Church, Charlotte, NC. She holds a Doctorate of Ministry from Gordon-Conwell Theological Seminary. Her dissertation emphasis was Spiritual Direction and Soul Care. She is also a graduate of Princeton Theological Seminary with a Master's Degree in Christian Education and a Bachelor's Degree in Clothing and Textiles from North Carolina Central University. In addition, she is a Sales Manager at Freedom Financial Advantage, LLC.

Barbara lives in North Carolina with her husband, Mr. Gilbert Peacock, and together they have a daughter, son-in-love, granddaughter, and grandson.

[BEGINNING OF CONVERSATION]

Renée: How do you support your wife's ministry calling to preach and teach God's word?

Gilbert: I have evolved into a position and role that ministry is not about me and is bigger than me. To a larger extent, I stay out of the way in terms of whatever she's trying to accomplish. I'm responsible from the standpoint of support. For the most part, when she has the opportunity to preach or teach, I try to be present in the congregation or audience so I can say "Amen" or "Hallelujah" or whatever to encourage her. Be the one that claps; lead off the clapping, because when people hear somebody clap, they tend to join in.

Renée: You used the word "evolve." Was it always that way?

Mr. Gilbert and Rev. Dr. Barbara L. Peacock

Gilbert: No, at the outset in 1991, we had moved from New Jersey to Michigan. After being there for a few months, she said she felt called into the ministry. With any change, it feels uncomfortable or abrupt, but you have to get past that. For me, I do what I usually do when I feel I don't know something—I consult a resource, whether it's a book, magazine, or someone who has experience or knowledge. So I called my uncle in California who is an Episcopal priest, and told him that Barbara said she's been called into the ministry. I asked him what he thought about that. We have a standing joke about him—he's so calm and mild mannered and is a pipe smoker. As if he was chewing on his pipe, he was silent for a while. He then came back and said, "What do you think about it?" I said, "The more I think about it, the only thing I hear is, 'let go and let God.'" So my interpretation of that came to mean that if God was really in this, then Barbara would go forward and be successful, but if God wasn't in it, He would sit her down and there would be obstacles or hurdles. So I figured I would let God do it and for me to get out of the way. I evolved to the point that it's bigger than me and not about me, which meant if He intends for it to work for her, He'll move the barriers and obstacles. In my case, I didn't want to be a barrier or obstacle and didn't want to feel that God would have to move me in order for her to be successful.

Renée: I can imagine that was a process?

Gilbert: Yes, it was over time.

Renée: How long would you say it took you to fully grasp that and accept it, not just intellectually and not just spiritually, but emotionally as a man, that your wife, your woman, is going to be out there, out front, preaching and teaching others, men and women, and you're going to be in the background in that setting? So emotionally, as a man, how did your ego deal with that, and how did you process that reality as a man, as the head of your house, as the head of your woman? How did you "feel" about that?

Gilbert: I didn't have any big reservations or big emotional feelings...I'm more analytical, more of a thinker. When you stress the thought that Barbara's "out front" and she's doing this and that, we're all products of our environment, products of what we see, and we learn and live. In my household, my mom and dad were married fifty years in 1991, and my mother was an educator for forty-one years in the public school system, and ten more years in community college. So fifty-one years she was on boards. She had a Master's degree and they were a great couple, great partners in marriage, in family and living, but at the same time, I called them the "odd couple" because of their credentials. Mom had a Master's degree and Dad had an 8th grade education. Long before women were accepted in ministry, my mom was called to speak at churches on Women's Day because she was an orator. She got to speak at three governor's inaugurations. So I saw that and lived with that. I've seen women's leadership out front. My dad was a cool, calm, humble, supportive guy. So it was easy. It wasn't about feelings—it was about what I had already lived, experienced, and what I had already seen.

Renée: It sounds like such an advantage in your situation with not having to grapple or struggle so very much with what God was doing in Barbara's life. That's wonderful.

Barbara: His only challenge was that it was his wife. But I want to go back to "Mama Peacock," as I think about the whole predestination of a man finding a wife, and God knows who He wants you to be compatible with. I think about when I first met "Mama Peacock," how I was impressed with her strength, her career, her ability to carry herself as a strong woman within a marriage, as a mother, her wisdom. At the time, I didn't know that I had a calling on my life. I was a young bride, twenty-five years old, but I admired her tremendously. So when I did accept my call, she was my greatest cheerleader. She was very supportive. My mother was raised in the traditional Baptist church, and she struggled because she had not been taught that women could minister, whereas Gilbert's mother was very supportive, and so when you asked him that question, I thought about that.

Gilbert: The other thing I would say is once I got to the notion in talking to my uncle, I kept thinking, "Let go, and let God." I said to her early on, "You need to get whatever credentials you need to get to make you credible," because with my mom being an educator, education was always stressed in our household. We all knew from day one that we were going to college. With Barbara and me in our household, it was stressed in our home with our daughter—it was always known you were going to college. It was the same with my older brother and his children. Part of your credentials, your education, gives you access, gets you in the door.

Barbara: When I started my ministerial career at The Park Church, back in the day when we joined in 1996 and I came on staff in 1999, people would say, "How did you get this job?" I would always point to my diploma. Of course, you knew God did it, but at that time, the pastor was really committed to hiring people that were theologically trained, and that was the foundation of The Park Church in the 1990's. But later on, he found he needed to balance that with business leaders and executives and started to diversify. I come from a family of strong education as well, so we both believe in education.

Renée: Yours sounds like an ideal situation based on your background, previous home environments—the influencers in your life. You were blessed to have some cheerleaders and encouragers early on. Everybody doesn't have that. What advice would you give, Gilbert, to other men whose wife is called into the ministry, and maybe they are struggling and didn't have what you have, and their experience is totally different, and they came to you—what emotional advice would you give that man?

Gilbert: I get the undertone that when you talk about soul care, that we are talking about emotions and feelings, but again I come back to the fact that I'm a thinker, I'm analytical—so from the standpoint of advice to an individual—and I'm talking to a male—and he says, "My wife is in ministry. How does that fall on you?" Basically, you share your own walk and your own experience and say, "Here's what we've done and this is what works for me." Basically, what works for me is that I have my own interests outside of what Barbara does as her career and ministry. Even though I have my own interests and purpose and calling, it still is good for you to be supportive of your partner and your mate...from the perspective of the Scripture, he who finds a wife finds a good thing and finds the favor of the Lord. To me, whatever levels that Barbara achieves or accomplishes within ministry and in her calling, that's all well and good because we all want to be enforced with the fact that we made good decisions. So whatever praise and glory and goodness and greatness and accomplishments that fall on her, there's some residual that comes back to me as well, simply because I chose her in the course of the marriage. It reinforces that I made good choice.

Barbara: I like that, Renée!

Gilbert: What gets me is the notion that "giving is living," and I'm known as being a giver. As much as you give as a giver, a lot of what you're accomplishing in the course of giving is making yourself feel good. While you may be meeting somebody else's need, you're still making yourself feel good. So while Barbara is being praised, or elevated, you can sit there comfortably and say, "Hey, I made a good choice. I married a smart person, somebody that can digest books, teach, preach, write...Look at what a good thing I did!"

Renée: She makes you look good.

Gilbert: I was looking up Proverbs 31 earlier, and in the course of this conversation, I captured several for the sake of this conversation. In addition to Proverbs 18:22, "He who finds a wife finds a good thing, and obtains favor from the LORD," I also emphasize the following verses:

- Proverbs 31:11 "The heart of her husband safely trusts her; So he will have no lack of gain."
- Proverbs 31:23 "Her husband is known in the gates, When he sits among the elders of the land."
- Proverbs 31:31 "Give her of the fruit of her hands and let her own works praise her in the gates."

Renée: Barbara, how do you, being the strong woman that you are, keep order within yourself—thus, in your home as a leader, as a wife, as a mother, as a woman, as your husband's friend, lover, the whole gamut...How do you keep all of that in balance?

Barbara: We got married in 1978 and moved to Connecticut in 1981. The first few years, you're newly married with a baby, and you do what you have to do. By the time you've settled in a couple of years, you ask yourself: "What's really going on here?" We had a good friend who was a peer mentor to us and also had a couple in Colorado in 1978 who mentored us when we got married. I remember taking the Family Life Conference early on in our marriage, and it talked about this umbrella. God was the head of the umbrella, and then the husband, and then the wife, and put them under it, under his sovereignty, thus, putting everything else in order. That simplified things for me to know what priority was. Even before that, when our daughter was about five years old, Gilbert used to travel a lot, and it was overwhelming for me. I had a business, and life was challenging. I had to look at the marriage and family picture and decide what I can and cannot do. One of our challenges was housework. We talked about it and made it possible, so that I could hire a housekeeper. If you're working and your husband is working, you have children and can afford it, you need to get help where you need help.

It is important to know that God is the Head and Covering of the house; your husband is the head and the priest of the home, and that your first ministry is your relationship with God. Then comes your relationship with your husband, and then your children, and everything else follows after that. Once you get that stuck in your head, the order becomes very simple. I was a Home Economics major in college, but ended up majoring in Fashion and Textile. I always believed in a healthy home as far as cleanliness, which I believe is next to godliness. Whatever you have is a gift that God has given you, and it is incumbent upon you to take care of it. Not only do you take care of your home, you take care of your car, and everything around you.

Then later on in our life, in the 80's we lived in New Jersey, and we came across something called the S.P.I.C.E.S. of life, which is an acronym for Spiritually, Physically, Intellectually, Career, Emotionally, and Socially. I added "Financially" later. What you do with the SPICES is rate yourself on a scale of 1 to 10 in each category. Back in the 80's, Gilbert and I would rate ourselves, and then rate one another. I use that chart all the time in my head. How am I doing spiritually? Am I physically fit? Am I aware of what's going on? How's my vocation? How's my emotional stability and my social relationships? How am I being financially astute? During mentoring relationships, the Bible is your foundation, and knowing the order of God's plan for the family and marriage and relationship is imperative. The SPICES of life is helpful and can be a tool that lets you know when you need help in a particular area. These are some of the things that have helped me along the way.

Gilbert: The only input I have on the chronology and the timing was in 1983 when we lived in Connecticut. Barbara was also going through a book called *You Can Be the Wife of a Happy Husband*. That was a spiritual book she went through with her friend. *The SPICES of Life* came out of Johnson and Johnson Corporation. We had a family friend who was an intern with them in the Health and Wellness department—that's where the SPICES of life were born in 1991, which was a milestone.

Barbara: It's one thing to have a spiritual foundation, but it's another to have practical application. Both the *Family Life Conference* book and *You Can Be the Wife of a Happy Husband* helped me know how to apply healthy principles to my life. Another book I studied fervently was *Becoming a Woman of Excellence.* Those were some of my foundational tools. I laugh when I read books now. I scan through them and make a note on the side, but back in the day, I would write out every Scripture, memorize them, try to interpret them and apply those Scriptures. I remember teaching a class at Mid Atlantic Christian Education Association, and they asked me to teach on *You Can Be The Wife of a Happy Husband.* It was a mixed group of women—black, white, and everybody else. Women were hanging out the door. There was no room anywhere. That was one of the most powerful classes I ever taught. We should have a class on that!

Renée: What encouragement would you give a woman regardless of her age, who is called to the office of minister and her husband is not as receptive as Gilbert was? If this man says, "no, I'm not having it!", but she knows she's called.

Barbara: Gilbert wasn't totally accepting early on. I do not want you to miss that part—he struggled. He was in management, and had this image to maintain that was important. Everybody wants to know what you do, what your wife does; they want to know your business. As a twenty to thirty something year old man, it was challenging to say, "My wife is a preacher." We did have those challenges, but when God touched his heart, he became the most supportive person ever. I'm not void of understanding the struggle women might have. What I would say about women whose husbands are having a struggle is to specifically pray for him. I remember in 1992 when I shared with Gilbert about this calling, he just couldn't see it. I kept trying to tell him and he wasn't receiving it. I felt like I needed to stop talking about it. I remember I was on my side of the bed praying, "God, I don't know how to get him to understand that you called me. I tried talking to him about it, and every time we talked, we'd end up in an argument, so what do I need to do?" I remember God telling me to get up from my side of the bed and go to his side of the bed and pray. When I got there, God said, "Now ask Me to show you how to serve him." So I went from trying to *tell* him to *serving* him. It wasn't long after that we went to this church in Michigan, and the pastor actually prophesied from the pulpit that I had a call on my life. When we got home, I told Gilbert the pastor was talking about me. Then Gilbert said, "Well I guess you need to go see the pastor." And that was evidence of what God can do if you just leave it alone. Because nobody can convince anybody of what God has called them to do or be. God has to show it to them if they don't believe.

Renée: And then you have to wait on God.

Gilbert: If the guy is struggling and the wife is called, what I think most men want in their relationship more than anything else is **respect**. So if from the perspective of the woman being called into the ministry, the man might be sitting there with the perception that now she's going to take me down off the pedestal and put our pastor/church upon the pedestal. Whereas, if you extend respect in your household in private, you'll extend respect in public, and that goes a long way. The early on advice that Barbara got from a pastor was that no matter the setting you go into or when you meet people, you turn around and say, "This is my husband." Make sure that your husband is introduced. In corporate, I always made sure she was introduced. I do that in almost all settings. If somebody new comes into a setting and I'm in a position to do so, I'll make sure that everybody else knows who that person is so that everyone knows everyone in the room. That's where you extend respect and inclusion. Those are two keys words...*inclusion and respect*. If you're going to shrink from honoring and respecting your husband simply because you have a calling, that God has called you and now it looks like you're putting somebody else up on a pedestal, there's going to be a struggle. It's the same with salvation. You can't preach your husband into nor coax him into salvation. God has to change his heart and his mind, because the biggest thing for a man in the course of accepting God as Lord and Savior is to know there's something on this earth that's greater and bigger than me. There are a lot of guys who are not willing to do that. They struggle with the notion of having Jesus Christ as Lord and Savior of their lives. So if you make him feel like there's something bigger and more important than him in your marriage and household, then yes, there's going to be a struggle. But if you always respect him in the home setting, church setting, and any other setting, it's probably going to be a whole lot easier.

Renée: Barbara, you were able to do that because you understood when God said to "serve him."

Barbara: Yes, we were living in Texas in 1993 and at that point, I was in the African Methodist Episcopal (A.M.E.) Church. I was sitting with my family in church, because I had already been licensed in Michigan. I said to the pastor that I wanted to sit with my family. He said, "Once you cross over, you don't go back." I said, "What?" That was an epiphany for me! So in 1996, God brought us here (to Charlotte) and we joined The Park Church, which was very active. I was talking to God about this ministry thing because I was in the pulpit all the time. I sensed God saying, "Where is the line? When do you make that shift?" It's like the pulpit is beyond the veil. But God said when you're in the pulpit, you're Rev. Peacock, but when you step down from the pulpit, you're "Mrs. Peacock." God always helped me to "shift." Not that you've stopped ministering, but you need to be more cognizant of what is happening around you. Family is always first! It's a challenge—it may not always look like it, but in your heart, that's the bottom line.

Gilbert: There's something that happens on both sides when it comes to the notion of *covering and protection*. One of your earlier questions was, "How can you be supportive when she's in a prominent role. How do you handle that?" So there are several roles in the course of a marriage. You're supposed to be a partner, a priest in the household, a provider, a protector. So even if she's in a ministerial role in or out of the pulpit and people are greeting her, it's wise counsel to be close by, be available, or be in arm's reach. That's part of your being a covering—to assist her by being there. And likewise, when she comes down out of the pulpit, if we are not in each other's orbit or proximity, then she's not in a position to protect her turf, either. Because if she's so caught up in ministry and I'm so far away, then that sets me up to be approached by other people or women. When she's ministering and people are coming up to her, then that sets her up to be approached by others or men. So there's a covering that applies to both that you need to be in each other's orbit and each other's sphere.

Renée: I like that. It's so clear and makes such sense that sometimes we miss it, because we tend to over spiritualize the calling. God doesn't expect you to no longer be the wife of Gilbert and Gilbert the husband of Barbara. It's almost that we become something else and are not being true to the first calling.

Barbara: Just think about it, if I'm in the pulpit, Gilbert not's going to come up and say, "It's time to go" or "let's go have dinner." But when I come out of the pulpit and people are greeting me and talking, I'm cordial, but at some point, you have to divide the line. We can look at each other and know that it's time to go. That "look" is not going to come when I'm in the pulpit, but when I step down. You have to know that and honor it. Then you begin to pull away, because people may not know how to separate the two, but you have to know.

Renée: Can you give me a definition of an emotionally healthy soul care provider in today's church or Christian community?

Barbara: I think the answer is in the question. A healthy soul care provider is first of all, someone who understands what soul care is. It's the attentiveness of a person in another person's life helping them discern the voice of God. I like the synonymous language of spiritual direction and soul care. They're used independently, but they can also be used interchangeably. The spiritual director knows that his or her job or calling is to be a conduit of attentively listening to the journey of another person and helping them see God in that. But in order for a person to be attentive to practice soul care and spiritual direction, then I believe and know they need to be healthy. I'm mindful of a book, *Sacred Slow: A Holy Departure from Fast Faith* by Alicia Britt Chole. She encourages the faith community, Christendom, the Christian church to slow down and to realize that God has called us first to be in relationship with Him. When I look for a healthy soul care provider, I look for someone who knows who they are in Christ, knows how to hear and listen to the voice of God, knows how to effectively listen to a directee or the person they are caring for, and takes the time to emotionally tend to their soul. And that requires rest, time, and things like keeping the Sabbath. I love the disciplines of the faith...detachment, attachment, rule of life... I believe a healthy soul care provider has a strong sense of emotional stability. I'm a big component of Peter Scazzero's book, *Emotionally Healthy Spirituality,* that talks about the lack of transparency of people in the body of Christ because they don't know who they are. In order to know who you are, you have to know who you are in the Kingdom.

Renée: Let me go back to something. You said keep the Sabbath. What do you mean?

Barbara: God tells us in the ten commandments in Exodus 20 that He gives us six days to work and the seventh day to rest. In His own model, He created the world in six days and rested on the seventh day. We celebrate the Lord on Sunday—that's the

Lord's Day. If you're in ministry, you're more than likely working on Sunday; so truly, you may not be able to have a Sabbath on Saturday, but to have a time of rest, slowing down, a time of being still, listening, meditating, contemplating, sleeping, or whatever you need to rest and be restored. David said, "He makes me to lie down in green pastures. He *restores* my soul." God knows we need help. He knows humanity needs a little nudging when it comes to rest. He compels me to lie down—to be by still waters. So a Sabbath—weekly, monthly—a sabbatical...I believe in all those disciplines that call us aside to rest.

I remember taking a sabbatical in 2005 while I was on staff at The Park Church. I did not get paid when I took my sabbatical, but God was calling me to rest. I already missed my Jubilee (when I turned fifty). Today, I think pastors are taking more advantage of sabbatical, Sabbath's rest. So when God called me to Gordon-Conwell Theological Seminary, I discovered this track called Spiritual Formation. After I read the description of this focus, I knew it had my name all over it. Therefore, I enrolled. I remember asking, *you mean there are people out there who really believe you're supposed to rest—to retreat?* And now God is doing it more and more in the church.

Renée: What do we do to obey God's command to remember the Sabbath and keep it holy, as the Sabbath is the seventh day, which is on a Saturday? Today in our contemporary world, Saturdays are, for the most part, full of everything but rest... chores, family, and children's activities, and then in the church, there are rehearsals, trainings, meetings...

Barbara: "I'm not going to the meeting."

Renée: What do you mean?

Barbara: It appears that the more "my church" can do, the more successful "my church" is. So the people are kept busy. When you look at Hebrews 4, it says that the children of Israel did not enter the Promised Land because they did not enter into God's rest. They didn't take time to stop and rest, didn't take time to be still and know that He was God (Psalm 46:10). It's a commandment even in the New Testament. Jesus rested. We have stories of Jesus resting...going to the mountains and getting away from the crowd to be with the Father. Even the religious leaders understood the Sabbath when they scolded Jesus about healing and doing other things on the Sabbath. They honored the Sabbath, but they were being legalistic about it. Jesus said not to be religious about the Sabbath, but to make sure you take time for Him to restore your soul...to be with Him. (Matthew 12:8, Mark 2:28, and Luke 6:5.)

Renée: So it may not necessarily be a Saturday.

Barbara: It means a day, a time—it may not be a Saturday because in our contemporary world, people work on Saturday; they work at night. That's why Jesus dealt with the Pharisees about their legalistic attitude about the Sabbath. God has given 168 hours in a week. You need to *take* the time, an hour, a day, a period of time. Because *not to rest is not to trust*. When I don't rest, I'm saying, "God, I can do it better than you can." I'm not trusting God to do it.

Look at it as a "mindset." It's a state of mind. It's doing something you enjoy alone or with your family and friends. It's a mental state of rest. Sleep—take the time to go away (physically or mentally), even throughout the day...it's a choice.

True rest gives your *body* a chance to recharge. It gives your *mind* a chance to get healthier. It gives you [your *spirit*] time to be intimate with God. It's almost a state of "nothingness." That's when you know you're really resting.

[END OF CONVERSATION]

I concluded my conversation with the Peacocks on the note of God's commandment to us as soul care providers who are pursuing optimum and holistic health. Remember to take your Sabbath's REST, as it is indeed holy unto God.

In the book Spiritual Disciplines Handbook - Practices That Transform Us, *Adele Ahlberg Calhoun directs us to consider REST a spiritual discipline.*

"God created us in his image. He is a God who works and then rests. When we rest we honor the way God made us. Rest can be a spiritual act-a truly human act of submission to and dependence on God who watches over all things as we rest....Rest is a radical thing in our day and age. It reminds us that we are human beings, not human doings. We are meant to live sane lives that partake of a deep and playful holy leisure. There is enough time in each day for all that God requires of us. And part of what He requires is rest. So settle in and breathe deeply of his gift of rest."

For more on rest, self-care, slowing, simplicity, silence and other disciplines that can enhance our holistic wellbeing, consider reading Spiritual Disciplines Handbook.

Suggested Resources

Gilbert Peacock—*www.freedomfinancialadvantage.com*

Books by Dr. Barbara L. Peacock

Psalm 119 Journal

C.A.L.L.E.D. To Teach

www.barbaralpeacock.com

Dr. Peacock recommends the following books and resources:

Emotionally Healthy Spirituality by Peter Scazzero

Sacred Slow: A Holy Departure from Fast Faith by Alicia Britt Chole

Keeping the Sabbath Wholly by Marva Dawn

Considerations?

_____

_____

_____

_____

_____

Confessions?

_____

_____

_____

_____

_____

Convictions?

_____

_____

_____

_____

_____

More Conversations?

_____

_____

_____

_____

_____

"If your heart is broken, your mind can't think straight and your spirit cannot soar."

—Adapted from *The Grief Recovery Method Handbook*

CHAPTER 6

EVERY SOUL CARE PROVIDER NEEDS A SOUL CARE PROVIDER

In Conversation with *Natasha Stewart*

NATASHA STEWART, M.A., LPC, currently serves as the director for The Center for Counseling and Behavioral Health at The Potter's House of Dallas, under the leadership of Bishop T.D. Jakes.

Natasha's passion, transparency, and authenticity has made her a sought-after keynote speaker, life coach, and counselor. Natasha has had the amazing opportunity to work with professional athletes and sports teams, politicians and governmental agencies, faith-based entities, as well as the nation's top universities and colleges.

Natasha has also appeared as a guest contributor on numerous television, radio, and social media platforms.

Natasha considers herself a lifelong learner and is inspired to share what life has taught her about the power of inner healing, hope, and new beginnings.

Her education includes:

- B.A. in Theology from Oral Roberts University
- M.A. in Counseling from Oral Roberts University
- Ph.D. in Society and Human Rights from Latin University of Theology
- Certified FOCCUS Counselor
- Certified Prepare Pre-Marital Counselor
- Certified Life Coach

Natasha is Mother of two, Kiana, a recent graduate of Dillard University, and Anthony, a sophomore at the University of Oklahoma.

"Where there is no counsel, the people fall, but in the multitude of counselors, there is safety"
(Prov. 11:14, NKJV).

[BEGINNING OF CONVERSATION]

Renée: How long have you served as Director of the Center for Counseling and Behavioral Health at the Potter's House, and how long have you been a professional licensed counselor?

Natasha: I started at the Potter's House in 2007 and actually partnered with the local hospital to have a faith-based unit at one of the psychiatric facilities here in Texas as the Assistant Director. I did that for about a year and then transitioned to the church where they had a full-service counseling center. I came aboard as the Assistant Director at the Counseling Center, and in 2009 became the Director. I was licensed in Oklahoma in 2000 as a licensed professional counselor and then moved to Texas in 2007.

Renée: As a counselor at the Counseling Center and even when you were in the faith-based unit at the hospital, what is the most glaring emotional deficit that you see in God's leaders—for example, pastors, chaplains, and anyone responsible for caring for the souls of others?

Natasha Stewart

Natasha: One of the most glaring deficits is they don't practice what they preach in terms of self-care and being holistic—taking care of mind, body, and spirit. When you listen to messages that come across the pulpit any given Sunday morning or turn on the television, you hear pastors giving messages essentially telling everybody else to take care of themselves spiritually, physically, financially...all the "llys," but I don't think they do a good job of doing it themselves. They sometimes feel immune to the challenges and problems of life, or maybe don't know how to deal with them correctly.

Renée: Where does that stem from?

Natasha: In the church world and the faith-based community, I think we have this misconception that pastors and leadership don't have struggles and don't face problems, but that everything is rosy and perfect, or God wouldn't call them. That's where we fail, and then leadership buys into that. Feeling that pressure, they wear these masks and have this cape and adopt the "superman" syndrome. But the truth is superman is "Clark Kent" too. We value "superman," but we overlook "Clark Kent."

Renée: And then God forbid if they show the "Clark Kent" side.

Natasha: They're going to be judged, humiliated, somehow lose their connection to God or their anointing from God. They're leading the sheep, but then they smell like sheep.

Renée: Not only does that pastor in those cases suffer from the superman syndrome, they might pass that along to the sheep, who then might have unrealistic expectations.

Natasha: Exactly, because then it trickles down to thinking that if my head [leader] is doing well and prospering and doesn't have challenges, and I'm sitting under them, then why am I having challenges, as I am under their teaching? What's going on with me? Why are these things happening in my life? So then I'm going to fake it till I make it; I'm not going to be honest.

One of the things I really respect Bishop Jakes for is his transparency and his establishing a counseling center as part of the church. He said across the pulpit on a Sunday morning that when God called him, he argued with God and said, "No, get one of those perfect people. I'm not perfect. I have all these flaws and insecurities and things I struggle with. Now looking back, I so wish those people I looked up to had been real with me, because I wouldn't have argued with God so long about calling me if I saw their imperfections and knew God used imperfect people."

Renée: Who can change that, and then once we determine who can, how then do we change that? We're in such a "code blue" situation right now. We've got younger people—the millennials, the mosaics, some of whom have lost faith in the church, in church leaders, especially when they see "Clark Kent." Whose responsibility is it to change the thinking, mindset, and thus behavior?

That's what Jesus did—He accepted people where they were, but loved them enough not to leave them there.

Natasha: We're all responsible for changing it. This is a weird thing that I'm about to say and I hope you'll understand. My grandmother used to say, "Life will teach you what you won't let me tell you." I think life is teaching the church what it won't listen to otherwise. With the younger generation leaving the church or those with church hurt, this exodus is forcing the church's hand to address these issues. Once we all accept responsibility, one of the ways to change is by having these conversations. This book, *What About Me?*, the counseling centers, pastors addressing it on Sunday morning, are just some ways to change. Just in the wake of these recent high-profile suicides with Kate Spade and Anthony Bourdain, pastors are coming across their pulpit about the subject. I saw several things on Facebook, Twitter, and other social media where they were saying that it's okay to talk to Jesus and a therapist. I think we're starting to hit that wall and knock it down. We can use the term "Berlin wall" in the church; we're starting to remove bricks of that wall. And once again, life is going to force you to talk about these issues. We cannot keep hiding. We're coming full circle. We have to accept people. That's what Jesus did—He accepted people where they were, but loved them enough not to leave them there.

Renée: The quote from your grandmother is such wisdom and she did not have a PhD. She had "mother wit."

Natasha: No, not a PhD nor a high school degree, but she used to say, "I don't have that theology you went to school to get, but I've got that "knee-ology." She got that wisdom by praying and talking to God.

Renée: As I was reading an article, the first thing noted is that pastors and spiritual leaders have left the position of prayer. Prayer is the way for us to get to that place of soul care that we need.

Natasha: The danger is when we go to prayer, we go in with preconceived ideas with what God is going to say and how He's going to say it. If your mind is shut off to mental health and emotional wellness, when you pray, you're not going to hear that, or you might hear it, but you'll ignore it. "I'm binding up the devil; he's trying to get in my mind." We have to be open. Talking about the deficit in leadership, some may believe they've arrived, that they've been on the mountaintop, and so if the former generation didn't need that, then we don't need it either.

I always caution pastors and leaders to be open. Never put God in a box, because once you can define God, He ceases being God. One of the axioms of God is that I can't define Him; I can't put Him in a box. And once I feel I have a cap on all His revelations, knowledge, and wisdom, I then make myself a god. I think that's why stuff is coming in the church the way it is—we have made religion more valuable than relationships. We say, "This is how we've done it and have always done it... we just need to pray." Well, there's something else. I believe in prayer; I want us to pray; we need to go back to prayer; but when we pray, we must pray with open hearts and minds to receive and hear what the Spirit is saying. He may say that you need to network with a counseling center, or see a therapist. You need to be aware of your emotional and mental health. When we pray, we don't need to be closed off.

Renée: I did a class on prayer once, and God had me to deal with the issue of "intelligent" prayers. How do we pray intelligently rather than as you said, closed minded prayer with a preconceived notion? I call it, going to God with our "God's To Do List."

Natasha: We're calling it prayer, but we're actually telling God what to do.

Renée: As a counselor, how do you care for your soul, because you're constantly giving out to care for the mind and soul of others? You're entering some dark and complex places. In addition, how do you care for the counseling staff?

Natasha: I have a therapist, a counselor, someone to go to when I need that safe space. I practice self-care, and I have really good boundaries. Boundaries are essential, especially when you're dealing with everybody else's problems. I can't take them home with me. I can't carry them. I can't be bigger than God. If God is allowing somebody to go through something, sometimes it's what we go through that makes us. I can't get in the way of their process. Sometimes as counselors, we want to help people, or stop the pain, or shorten the process for them. I can't do that. I have to leave their stuff in the office. When I close my door for the day, all their stuff stays in my office. I have a safe place. I have a good supportive network of friends that allow me to be me.

On Saturdays twice a month, I do a mentoring, and one of the things I told them this past Saturday was that a sign of maturity is accepting a person as they really are, not how you hope or wish them to be. I have two people in my life that have known me for years. They have seen the good, the bad, and the ugly. They've seen the spiritual side, the not so spiritual side of Natasha. They get Natasha. You have to have people in your life that hold you accountable and that you're accountable to—someone you can really let your hair down with and be honest with. That's what's lacking in our lives. We don't have people we can be honest and truthful with and share our secrets with.

That's why counseling is so important because it gives you that. When you walk out of that office, you're still whoever you are when you walked in. There's no judgment, no shame, no guilt—and that's why I say people who go to counseling are the luckiest people in the world because how many of us have a safe place? Think of it in those terms. A lot of people like to put a negative connotation on counseling. I say, no, they've got counseling all wrong. That's the one place I can go and be completely me without any judgment, and then get tools and skills that help me to be the better version of myself and erase "stinking thinking."

People who go to counseling are the luckiest people in the world because how many of us have a safe place?

Renée: I do lay counseling. I'm not a licensed professional counselor, but I am certified as a grief recovery specialist. I had never looked at counseling that way—that they are so lucky to have one, of course assuming it is a good counselor.

Would you say that education and awareness is paramount?

Natasha: Most definitely. Because when we know better, we do better. I think we've lacked education. For a long time, that was a fight in the church, being educated and going to school. We've come a long way with that. I think we're on that spectrum of arming ourselves. The more knowledge we have, the better. The Bible talks about having wisdom and knowledge. It is paramount, and it is key, and the more we understand mental health and emotional wellness, the better we'll get at it.

Renée: One of the participants in the conversations is a psychiatrist who is a believer. She does talks to churches and pastors from a mental health perspective and education. What those believers who are professionals and understand the holistic approach to healing can do is bring that to the church, use what God has given them, use that in the church, and pray that the pastor will be open and receive it.

Natasha: Exactly what you're saying, those of us who are believers coming in and teaching people because there is so much stigma, myths, and fallacies that if we had that educational component and show them that God is concerned about our mental health and emotional wellbeing and it's in the Bible. God talks about being a Wonderful Counselor and that there is safety in counseling. I think it would change the conversation and open up doors.

Renée: What do you do for your staff? How do they take care of themselves?

Natasha: I encourage them to see a therapist. I went to Oral Roberts University where I got my Master's Degree, and one of my professors, before we graduated said, "Every good counselor has one." That always stuck with me. I encourage them to have self-care and not to leave any vacation days on the table. You have them for a reason. You don't owe me an explanation—just give me notice. And sometimes you have a morning when you wake up and say, I need a personal mental health day myself. We have within the counseling center a really good support system. They have said, "You are the first boss or supervisor that's more than a supervisor." I allow them that space, and I tell them as long as you all can handle me having multiple roles in your life, we can do this. Sometimes they need a supervisor, but sometimes they need a safe place. They may say, "I'm struggling with relationship issues, or how do I believe God for this?" Every Friday, we have prayer—before we open our doors to clients or our daily activities, we come together and pray. That has made us closer, and it develops trust. We carry one another's burdens as the Bible says to do.

Renée: How would you address the professionals in the church who are therapists, psychologists, nurses, and others in the helping field with respect to using their profession in ministry in light of dual relationships, and even state laws? How can they use what God has given them in the church without violating the professional laws?

Natasha: It's the way we look at it. This is my opinion. The professional may think, "I do this at work—I don't want to come to church and still work." People really have to see it as a ministry. It's who I am. Just as I am a black woman everywhere I go, I can't separate that. I can't turn it off; I can't change it. I think sometimes when you're called to this, the counseling, therapy, helping, you can't turn it off. If we do it 9 to 5, we can't turn it off when we're in the choir stand or sitting in the pew. However, you do have to develop a way where you're not breaking ethical laws.

One of the ways I do that with people I have a ministry relationship with is I tell them, "I can be your life coach, but I can't be your therapist. I need you to know the difference." I get them to sign a statement where they are not receiving counseling from me, but I can point them to a place where they can get counseling. They may not always come to me, but I can be a vessel. I can tell them I may not be the person to talk to because it's a dual relationship; we sing together; we worship together. But I can refer you to someone who can help you. It's important to develop a referral network.

Renée: We just don't want to "dump" that person.

Natasha: There are levels of holding your hand, of walking through something with people. We're called to do that, but I don't go over my scope or my ability. I take you as far on the journey as I can, and then I hand you over to competent people to help you the rest of the way. As they help you, it doesn't mean that I lose touch with you or I don't follow up with you, but they are going to be invested in your journey from here on out as well.

Renée: I assume I know the difference between a counselor and a life coach, but give me your definition of a coach. What is coaching in this context versus counseling?

Natasha: To me, coaching is very specific. Counseling is going to cover your life—what happened in childhood. It's going to be very clinical and have a therapeutic value. Coaching is what's going on right now and how I can help you in this moment. I can give you some resources and suggestions, and then maybe give you a referral to someone if there is a deeper psychological issue that's going on. I'm not going to get clinical, for example, "How was your childhood?" or "Was there any abuse or mistreatment?" With coaching, its more goal directed. Counseling is too, but if you want better performance on your job and need to build better relationships with your co-workers, then I will give you very practical ways to do that. Now if you come to me in counseling with that, I'll ask, "Have you always had problems with relationships in childhood? Were there abandonment or detachment issues?" I'll go deep with you. Coaching is surface, but still has value. A good coach, once they see they hit those things and that there are deep underlying issues, will not just treat it as a "fix it" type situation. They'll refer them to somebody else they can talk with to help explore why they're having trouble handling relationships. It's deeper that what my level of involvement on relationships in your life can handle.

Renée: Can you share an instance where you had to take some of your own medicine? Where you found that if you didn't do something, you may go off the edge/deep end or that you were stuck? If that has happened in your life, what did you do?

Natasha: I was married for eighteen years and then went through a divorce. It made me very aware of separating what I do from who I am because I have cards, letters, emails saying, "You're just the best," "You saved our marriage," "You changed our lives," etc. Yet, I'm coming home and my marriage is in shambles. How can I be the Director of the Potter's House Center for Counseling and getting all this other stuff right, but I can't get it right in my house? So I realized, I'm an individual too, and that's when I knew I need to go find a counselor, talk to somebody, and sort this out. I need to practice self-care because I'm not being taken care of in this relationship. Now I have to do what I have to do so that me and my children are taken care of—that we're healthy emotionally, physically, mentally, and spiritually. I know there's a lot of controversy in the church about divorce. But that was my answer. I can honestly say that being invested after eighteen years, I didn't do it lightly. But like I tell others in counseling, you can't change another person. You don't have that much power. I had to take that medicine myself. I can't make someone want what I want or do what I want. This is not working and no matter how much effort, it takes two people to save something. If they repeatedly make wrong choices, how long do I cover to the point where my own mental or emotional health is at jeopardy? That period of my life made me look at what I was telling everybody else. If someone was going through what I was going through, I wouldn't have made the choices I made. I had to be very honest with myself. If this was your daughter, your client, you wouldn't advise them to do this. So why are you doing it? Part of it was that mask, "I'm the Director of the Counseling Center at the Potter's House. I have to look like I have it all together. Who's going to come to me when I'm going through a divorce? How am I going to explain this to my bosses and they're like, "Don't you specialize in counseling?"

It was a day of reckoning, but I can tell you when I left out of that courtroom, it felt like 600 pounds had been lifted off my shoulders. I walked out so free. I knew I had made the right decision. It's been six years and I have never doubted, never regretted, never questioned that decision. My life has improved so much. It's amazing. It happened at the right time.

Renée: Were there children involved?

Natasha: I have two children. At the time, they were sixteen years old and thirteen years old.

Renée: How are they now?

Natasha: They are good. That was my concern, too. I said, "God, you've got to cover my children." A lot of why I stayed was because I didn't want them to grow up in a broken home. I didn't want their father not to be present in their lives. For a lot of reasons, I stayed because of them, but on the flip side, I left because of them. I didn't want them to think this was normal and healthy and that this is what marriage looked like. I had to be honest and age-appropriate with them about my decision. What I was telling everybody else about trusting and believing God, I had to trust God to be the "gap filler" with my children. What gaps I couldn't fill in for them and what questions I couldn't answer for them, I needed God to do that. It's amazing that they both at separate times came back to me and said things to me that made me know that they were okay. I offered counseling to them—I didn't force it, but I told them, "I could set it up. If you don't want to go, you don't have to." They both opted not to go. I had to be very open, honest, and transparent with them. I did periodic checks with them. Now, my son is in his second year of college and he's a psychology major. At first he was going for engineering, but after taking a psychology class as a general class, he kept calling me asking questions, and then finally said, "I think I want to do this." I told him to pray about it and if God is leading you in that direction, then do it. He eventually changed his major. One of the things I'm so proud of is my relationship with my children. It's God! We have very good healthy relationships; they're able to talk to me. I remember my daughter's freshman year in college. As a communications major, she called me to tell me they were assigned topics to write about. Her topic was "divorce." I'm bracing for what she was going say. She said she used the analogy of a sports team. For a while, she thought I had just quit the team. But then she realized after the divorce how happy I was and how our lives had improved. She said, "You didn't quit the team; you just changed teams; you're still in the game." She said, "Mom, I'm so proud of you for finding your team and choosing to be happy!" That brought me to tears.

If we say we believe God, we just have to wait, and trust God. I realized that God had my children. Then later, with time, my son said something similar to me that my daughter had said.

God is the gap filler, but they are in His hands—they belong to Him. I said to God: "I'm not perfect, but you're a perfect God. You held my babies, and I thank you for that."

Renée: I'm hearing the term "gap filler." Waiting, that's the hard part most times. So let me ask you about your children. There is such an assault on the minds and emotions of our children: emotional, mental, physical distress, trauma due to violence, substance abuse, sexual assault, loss of safety, in person and online bullying. School shootings are sadly more commonplace that not. The list goes on and on. Recently, you experienced a school shooting in your state, San Diego, Texas. All of this can instill and breed fear. What do you say to the church today in addressing the souls of people, especially the souls of our children? How do we embrace this as our problem?

Natasha: We have to be real. We have to talk about these relevant topics as you've listed. Talk about gender identity issues, social media, and what is and what is not appropriate. We sometimes play patty-cake with nice safe things. "Did you accept Jesus as Lord and Savior? Do you love God and Jesus?" But what does that look like when you're at school and everything in the school is against your value system? How do you stand? I don't think we talk about or prepare our kids for real life. I think that's why they're leaving, because they don't think the church of God really addresses real life. It's something we do on Sunday morning, but it's not a lifestyle.

Renée: So they don't feel adequately prepared for the onslaught.

Natasha: Exactly. That's what I tell so many parents that come in. In recent years, more parents have come in about their child's confusion with their sexual identity and with gender identity issues. They were in an uproar: "I raised them in the church and we don't believe that." I get that. I do understand that. I am a Christian and I believe the Word of God, what the Bible says. I also believe in *love*, the power of love. I said, "If you turn your back on your child or family member, where are they going to go? They will go to the world, and the world is going to tell them, 'we love and embrace you just as you are.'" I say to them, "It's not your job to change your child. It's your job to give your child to God and let Him change them." He says He changes through loving kindness with which He draws us. It's your job to parent them and to love them and nurture them. If you eliminate your voice from their life, who are they going to listen to? Love doesn't mean agreement. Loving your child doesn't mean you agree with their lifestyle. It says that I love you no matter what.

I've been doing this since 1993. The stories I hear are about being separated from their child, and family members whose lifestyle they didn't agree with, and the heartbreak of the broken relationship that ensues. I seldom hear about loving them, anyway. I do hear about realizing they made the wrong decision when they cut off their child because they didn't agree with their sexual orientation, or any other lifestyle, or behaviors.

I ask that parent, "Do you love your child? Don't be their judge; don't be their god. If you judge and separate yourself, then they are no longer exposed to your love and Christian values, but they see judgment." I don't hear the story that "it was the best thing that I cut myself off from my child's life." I don't hear that, but I do hear regret that they did.

All these issues about life—even though you don't agree with it, it's not up to me to agree, it's up to me to love you. What does love look like? If we look at Christ, that's our model and example.

What is the proper representation of Christ? Look at what he did for us. The Bible says that "while we were are yet sinners, Christ died for us" (Rom. 8:5).

While you're yet a homosexual, a liar, a sinner, or whatever, I can love you. I think in the church, we don't talk about that; it's *either, or*. It can't be *and or with*. We categorize sin as big sins and little sins. Sexual identity, drugs...those are those big sins. So you lie, you cheated on your taxes...ah, those are little sins!

I ask the question, "Tell me what amount of blood did it take to save you versus saving a homosexual? Did it take more blood to save the homosexual than you?" We rationalize our sins and judge everybody else's. So while you rationalize your sin, did it take a drop for you and a whole pint of blood for someone else's sin? Tell me when Jesus died, did it take just one nail for you and three nails for someone else's sin? We don't have those discussions in the church.

Renée: Was His blood not good enough for sins we have categorized as worse than ours?

Natasha: So when we talk about our youth and the stuff they have to deal with today, they don't need a judgmental church and a legalistic litany of do's and don'ts and what's right and wrong, because we have an innate sense of what's right and wrong. What we need is *love*. God said He drew us with lovingkindness. Once I know you love me, then I can hear from you and you can then speak into my life. But if I think you're just judging me, analyzing me, critiquing me, then I don't allow you to speak into my life. I shut you down before we can ever have the conversation. So if we want to reach our youth, we have to stop with the judgment and coming at them as if we have all the answers. All I have is Christ. The disciples told the man at the temple, "Silver and gold have I none, but what I do have I give you" (Acts 3:6 NKJV).

What I have is the love of Christ. He loves us just as we are, but He loves us way too much to leave us there. When we start this journey, it's not a judgment journey, it's a love journey. I find even with my kids when I love them through stuff, they do better. That doesn't mean not holding people accountable, because love holds people accountable. You can say anything to anybody, but it's how you say it.

Renée: Since we're talking about our children and young people, before we close, it's mentioned in your bio that you speak to and work with professional athletes, sports teams, politicians, etc., as well as universities and colleges. Have you worked with college chaplains or student Christian associations on college campuses?

Natasha: I have not worked with chaplains. But that's interesting that you ask that. Usually with universities, the counseling centers or the coaches will reach out to me. I ask them why they are reaching out to me? So that counseling center or the coaches will call, but I have yet to have a spiritual life director or campus chaplain reach out to me.

Renée: I see that as a need, because so many things are happening on campuses with the young minds, brilliant minds, and with their spirits and bodies. They are subject to an onslaught of a myriad of attacks including date rape, the occult, and other philosophies that sound good, but are not of Christ. I've had personal experiences with young adults who are suffering with mental health and emotional issues that became very evident while in college.

Natasha: Statistically, that's when people experience their first psychotic breakdown is in that age group. Historically and culturally, African Americans seek out spiritual advice before we did anything else.

Renée: With that said, how can colleges, Bible colleges, and seminaries better prepare someone who is going into the ministry when it comes to emotional and mental health of the souls they'll be "watching" over?

Natasha: My personal recommendation is that they all have to get a counselor. They would have more classes in that field and have to get the CEU's (Continuing Education Units). Just as doctors have to do a rotation in psychiatry, they would have to do that and then talk about that. The best thing is firsthand experience when you, yourself sit and talk to a counselor. I would make it mandatory to have six sessions with a counselor.

People don't know how freeing it is when you have a "safe space" to come and say whatever. However, if you don't do it, haven't seen it, don't believe in it, then it's hard to offer it to somebody else.

Renée: I've heard through first hand conversations and statistics, when one comes out of seminary or Bible college, they are really not prepared to deal with emotional and mental issues that will naturally come their way. They know how to exegete the text and be homiletically astute, but not necessarily how to work in the trenches of ministry to the soul.

Natasha: Exactly, they're not really equipped, especially when you experience life issues within your own soul.

Renée: "If your heart is broken, your mind can't think straight and your spirit cannot soar."

Adapted from *The Grief Recovery Method Handbook*

This quote brings to mind Bishop T. D. Jakes' book, *Soar*. On the back cover, Bishop Jakes encourages the reader:

"Flight is possible even for those who are emotionally, financially, and creatively fatigued. You can take your vision, build it into something remarkable, and reach heights you could have never imagined."

What counsel would you give to the leader who is emotionally fatigued or feels emotionally incapable? They want to do what is laid out in *Soar*, but they can't seem to even read the "flight plan."

Natasha: I would ask, "Why? Why are you emotionally incapable? If you have the desire to do it, then you can do it." There is a process in doing it, but I would want to know the lie that tells you, "You cant." You may have some challenges and you might do it, but not like the next person is going to do it. But you can do it. So I need to figure out why you are coming at it with the notion that you can't. What do we need to eliminate from your life or add to your life so that you can?

Renée: So that you can soar.

Natasha: Yes, because you have been cleared for "takeoff."

[END OF CONVERSATION]

Considerations?

_____
_____
_____
_____
_____
_____

Confessions?

_____
_____
_____
_____
_____
_____

Convictions?

_____
_____
_____
_____
_____
_____

More Conversations?

_____
_____
_____
_____
_____
_____

MEDITATIONAL SOUL NOTE

"If you don't handle your pain, your pain will handle you."

—Bishop Joey Johnson

CHAPTER 7

A PARADIGM SHIFT

In Conversation with *Bishop Joey Johnson*

PRESIDING BISHOP F. JOSEPHUS JOHNSON, II, better known as Bishop Joey Johnson, is the Organizer and Senior Pastor of The House of the Lord in Akron, Ohio.

Bishop Johnson is a renowned Bible scholar, counselor, educator, conference speaker, and workshop facilitator. His experience in leading one of the city's largest churches for forty-four years has equipped him to impart wisdom for issues related to church growth and development, business management, leadership, and team building.

As a visionary, Bishop Johnson founded The Johnson Leadership Institute, where he utilizes his skills to train and mentor pastors and other church leaders. As a lover of the Holy Scriptures with keen intellectual curiosity and insatiable appetite for reading, Bishop Johnson founded Emmanuel Christian Academy and Logos Bible Institute to present opportunities to children and adults to be educated and equipped in God's Word.

As Bishop Johnson increasingly ministers to the community of faith, not only in the city of Akron, but around the world, his participation and influence in the community continues to grow on so many different levels One example of this is his commitment to attacking and solving the problem of poverty in our city. To do this, Bishop Johnson continues to humbly invite city and state leaders to sit at the same table. He is careful to reject the role of a hero, while he has embraced, with the good of all in mind, the role of being a host of conversations.

Bishop Johnson authored nine books, *The Church: The Family of Families*; *God Is Greater Than Family Mess*; *The Eight Ministries of the Holy Spirit* and *The Eight Ministries of the Holy Spirit Study Guide*; *The Biblical World Through New Glasses*; *Lord of the Flies: A Leadership Fable*; *Grief - A Biblical Pathway to God*; *The God Who Grieves;* and *The Ravages of Rejection,* published August, 2017.

Bishop Johnson is married to Pastor Cathy Johnson.

PART 1 - THE DYNAMIC CALL, PREPARATION, AND EMOTIONAL READINESS OF THE SOUL WATCHER

Renée: Hebrews 13:17 is glaring. It indicates that the senior pastor is the chief soul care provider in the church. God says, "Obey your spiritual leaders, and do what they say. Their work is to watch over your souls, and they are accountable to God" (NLT). Tell me what God expects of you?

Bishop Johnson: The gist of what's going on begins in the very first word. Many who study the verse only go so deep and do not determine the level of relationship being exhorted. The word "obey" is typically interpreted to obey as a child, which would determine the relationship out of which the soul watch is taking place. The word does not mean to obey as a child. One of the Lexicons says to obey as an adult who has spent time learning and getting to know the father's heart. Not obey as a child, but as a healthy adult child. The context of the soul care is not to obey me as a child, but as a father would continue to mentor a loving son. The context of the soul care is a healthy relationship.

Renée: How does that happen?

Bishop Joey Johnson

Bishop: It starts first with the person who is doing the caring. The one who has the most responsibility needs to make sure they're caring for themselves, and that is often where we miss the boat. Often in America, we are so intent with equipping people to help other people from an academic perspective. We often do not require those people to move towards their own health. We're simply trying to equip them to do a job, rather than mentoring them and growing them so they can be who God has called them to be. This is the context from which the job can take place.

It's not a job first, but a calling. A calling indicates a spiritual reality that goes beyond simply some characteristics that one needs to manufacture or to educate.

Renée: Does that explain when God talks about bishops, senior leaders, pastors in the church, and says, "Lay hands suddenly on no man?"

Bishop: The verse deals with the bishopric, the deacon (the diaconate). It deals with the list of characteristics, first of the person being ordained or elected. We skip those rather rapidly to get to what the person is going to do, but it starts out with who the person is—the husband of one wife or one wife at a time, and then it goes down to being temperate. When you add all those characteristics up, you're talking about somebody who is mature, somebody who is healthy. We no longer have that requirement for pastors.

Seminary is generally a hermeneutic and homiletic factory to teach you how to interpret, teach, and preach the text, which is not bad, because it's part of the calling. But pastoring is not just preaching—preaching is a gift that God has given. Pastoring is shepherding; it's not simply feeding.

Renée: When those who feel they're called to pastor go to seminary or Bible college, or they don't go at all, what would you change so they're better prepared? What needs to happen so they can **be** who you just described, and whose soul is healthy enough to watch for the souls they will shepherd?

Bishop: One of the problems that hinders adequate preparation is the separation of the Academy from the Church. At one time, if we go back far enough in history, particularly in Biblical history, your son already knows what he is going to be because he is part of a family that pursues a particular calling. You're therefore mentored from the time you're born to be able to do what you're called to do. In that mentoring, you have a personal relationship with someone who is molding you and helping you grow up to where you're going and who you are going to be. With the Enlightenment and other things, we've separated the Academy from the Church. Now we're sending people to school to be educated, sometimes by professionals who may not be connected to the church where they need to go back to minister. Therefore, we've created a discontinuity between the place of ministry and the place where education is taking place for ministry. So that needs to be returned in some format to the church where that ministry is taking place, whether through practicum or through more pastors and preachers doing this.

The Academy is recognizing right now that many people who are going back to school are bi-vocational. They're no longer just a student going to class to get a grade but a pastor who works during the day. They are going to school after work where they're trying to further their skills and their craft. That is dictating a change in how things are being done because of that lack of connection with the leader and the mentoring factor.

Renée: You see that trend.

Bishop: Yes, it's going on right now. People aren't going to seminary at the rate they once were, and more older pastors are now going. The problem is that the previous delivery system is geared for academics and students who are young. Whereas now, we have fifty-year-olds trying to augment what they're already doing, so the delivery system must be re-designed.

Renée: Why is a fifty-year-old who is already pastoring going to school? What is going on now?

Bishop: They didn't have a mentor; they don't have many friends; therefore, they don't have any support or training, so they recognize they need help. Where do I go to get that help? And since they're not healthy enough to go to a pastor or somebody that they might consider to be a competitor and get help, they are going back to the institution to find help. So it's causing people who are much older than the traditional student in the past to be in the classroom.

It's also an issue of money. Schools are recognizing enrollment is declining. Who should we target? We're targeting the wrong people. So we have to target those more likely to come to school to find out what are they looking for. Less and less are we seeing those in their late teens, twenty and thirty-somethings who are looking in a singular path to become a pastor, but more pastors already who are looking to augment their training.

Renée: So in respect to God's call, are younger people, both men and women in their twenties and thirties looking to fulfill the call on their life in some other way rather than being a pastor?

Bishop: This is an excellent question, but it impinges on our entire society where we have the Mosaics or Millennials. This age group is very unique, and some don't see the church as viable, and therefore are not using that particular pathway. They are going into all kinds of things, but not necessarily the ministry, which is causing a re-evaluation. So what do we need to do if we're going to survive?

I'm partnering with Ashland Theological Seminary to create what we've called a certificate of ministry program. It is a Bachelor's level training program in conjunction with the University designed to be practical that will allow you to achieve a certificate in two to four years. You'll then be able to go directly into their Master's program and be Bachelor's exempt, except the training is not taking place at the Academy, but is taking place in the church. And more practitioners are participating in this type of training rather than traditional Academic.

We've been doing this about two to three years, and it is working very well. I usually have twelve to fifteen students working on their certificate. They're being mentored and helped, and are learning in a practical classroom setting, and yet we're still covering the Academics, but not from a "Greek" perspective which entails a "write this on the test" perspective, but more practically, "How do I work these things out?" perspective. There are many people who can write it on the test, but they can't do it.

Renée: So does that include having an assigned ministry role or involvement in a church?

Bishop: Generally, we haven't set that requirement because many of those in the certificate program are already in ministry. They are already working, trying to figure out how to get help. Their problem is they can't go back to school full-time at the Academy. So this is a much more practical pathway for those particular people to become equipped.

Renée: Do you see the Mosaics/Millennials participating?

Bishop: We do have some participating, but they are rather on the end because it's much more vocationally driven. They are working in the church and may have another job or something else, but they are interested in transferring into the church environment. I have two or three young men who have secular jobs, but want to learn how to teach the Word of God. God has called them to pastor, but they don't know when or where. They want to be equipped, but realize they can't do that in a university.

Renée: With that, let's look at that young man or woman who is married and even with children. How do they balance this? Otherwise, something is suffering and elements for unhealth are there. How do we maintain emotional health and balance?

Bishop: We have to go back and re-do or undo some things. We're applying an American paradigm to a Biblical context. Once again, we're teaching people achievement rather than helping them to understand what God's calling is in their lives. It's not a simple calling; it's not one calling, but there are multiple callings and multiple covenants that need to be considered. You have a calling to be a citizen in this society; a calling to be a husband or a wife; a calling to be a father or mother; a calling to be a pastor, or whatever. What we've done is taken the spiritual calling and elevated it above all other callings.

So what has occurred is an imbalance, because we're making that which is spiritual more important than anything else.

I'm doing a sermon series on connecting Sunday worship to Monday work. We spend forty to sixty percent of our time at work, and five percent at corporate worship, yet, when I come to church, we never talk about work. We only talk about worship and God and spiritual perspectives, but we don't know how to connect them. The average person doesn't understand how to connect that back to my job. The fact is that I have a calling on my job. From the book of Genesis, it would seem that your first calling is to your job. God created us to create something and put us in the Garden of Eden and said to till and guard it. That's where you start. It doesn't mean you don't have a spiritual calling, but it means that your callings are many, and your covenants are many.

I teach something that most people have never heard of because the American paradigm doesn't allow us to think in these particular perspectives, and that is "colliding covenants." We try to prioritize our lives with a simple numeric system.

- Number one is God.
- Number two is my mate.
- Number three is my children.

I wish that life worked that way and it was that simple, but it's not. So if I make God number one, how much time should I give Him...sixty percent? Fifty percent? If I make my spouse number two, then how much time do I give them? And if I give my mate the kind of time I should, where do I take it from? If my children are number three...and so on. That's a numeric ideological system which does not work in practicality because you end up with "colliding covenants." You have a covenant with God and a covenant with your spouse; a covenant with your children; a covenant with your church; a covenant with others in your sphere of influence. So you see how I am enumerating the covenants, we're out of balance to begin with. Your covenant with God is not your covenant with your church or with your spiritual gift within the church. We've gotten that confused. I look at "colliding covenants" not like priorities on a list, but like planets in a solar system. Planets in a solar system revolve around a sun and have gravitational impact upon each other. It's a very complex dynamic system.

God is at the middle. He's impacting my priorities with my spouse, which impacts my priorities with my children, which impacts my priorities with my church. So there comes a time when I have to make a choice when my covenants collide. There comes a time when I have to decide. Do I pray this morning? Do I go to church for a prayer meeting? Do I take my wife for her doctor's appointment? They are colliding covenants, and we don't have any of that teaching or practicality. What little talk is given to it is a numeric flat priority system, which doesn't teach anybody anything. So we go out and struggle and try to figure out how to do it little by little, and get in trouble because we don't understand how they should be prioritized in the first place and how dynamic they are.

Renée: You probably need to write a book on "colliding covenants," because this is not a typical concept. It is definitely a paradigm shift in thinking. I love the analogy of the solar system. Help me understand the practical working out of the colliding covenants.

Bishop: We need to move from a production orientation to a "being" theology.

Production orientation in America has us constantly trying to figure out what we need to *do,* whereas "being" theology helps to try to figure out who we need to *be*. And when I am what I need to *be*, what I need to *do* will flow out of my being. In America, we try to have our being flow out of our doing.

We're constantly trying to do something to be something. I teach people that *living in a garage won't make you a car.* Doing something will not necessarily make you be something. Now it can if you do it long enough, if you're giving your whole life to it, but that's more than doing. That begins to hinge on being. The center of who I am revolves around God, revolves around His Word, and then that is lived out in a trial and error basis, and that's why we have trouble. We're people who are trying to get these priorities straight. I need to know what I should do first and what should I do second. Well that depends on your life, your life situation, where you are in your marriage, how long you've been married, how many children you have, your home of origin, your love language—it depends on a lot of things. It becomes a trial and error journey rather than a system of teaching.

Renée: And that takes time.

Bishop: It takes time! It takes relationship time. It takes sitting with God—doing all the things we don't do because we're production oriented. I need to produce this so I can produce that so I can move here, rather than I need to BE who God called me to be. It is being and becoming, not just doing. Now Jesus talked to the Israelites about doing because they were a being society. We take what He says about doing and re-transmit it to a doing society and then do more doing. So we don't understand that was a "being" society. At some point, He had to urge them towards doing, because they feel like to "be" is all that I need to do. I don't need to do any "doing."

For instance, there's a parable where Jesus asked the question that illustrates what's going on. We have no idea what He's talking about because we're American. He speaks about the father who has two sons. One son comes and says that he will do the will of the father, but he doesn't. The other son comes in and says he won't do the will of the father, but he does. Which one is doing the will of the father? That's an asinine question to us. It's very simple too—it's the one who does the will of the father. But not in the Hebrew culture. In the Hebrew culture, you don't have to do anything. If you honor your father's will, it's as good as doing it.

So we don't understand that, and we end up with a bunch of production-oriented actions. We then begin to get into commandments and try to please God from a legal perspective, rather than walk with Him as a son or a daughter. Back to Hebrews 13:17—obey your leaders; walk with them as somebody who spent time learning their heart.

Renée: You talk about the American culture and the Hebrew culture. Living in the contemporary Western world, and thus the Western way of processing what we learn, how do we adopt the Hebrew thought or even recognize that's a problem when we're trying to obey and understand God?

Bishop: First, all theology is contextualized. Whatever you're reading, you're reading it through somebody's lens. We've not been taught that, so we think we can pick the Bible up like a newspaper and read it. We don't know that it was written 2,000 years ago to a different culture, a different time, a different logic, and a different language. Even though we know that intellectually, we've not been taught it enough to work it out practically. So we still read it like a newspaper. The first thing I teach people in my training and mentoring programs is if you're reading the Bible and it makes sense to you, it's a good chance you don't know what it's saying. It shouldn't make any sense at all because it wasn't written to you—even though it was written for you, it wasn't written to you. Therefore, you have to understand what the original message was to the original people in its original time, so I can make an application to today. So we're in trouble out of the gate because we're trying to read the Bible as if it was written to us, and rather than being a principle book, we think it is a commandment book. So we're looking for hard and fast rules, a rule book rather than a relational book that sets out principles. We start trying to do what the rules are and try to be right rather than be in a right relationship.

So it's a whole paradigm shift.

Renée: This is a broader perspective of thought and reinforces the goal of this book, which is to incite, not indict. I hope the reader will pause as I just did and think, "What did he say?"

Bishop: All of that goes back to how you view God with all theology being contextualized. If you view Him as a judge, that will be one kind of a relationship. If you view Him as a father, that's a different kind of relationship. If you view Him as a doctor, as a Healer, that is a different kind of relationship. If you can see Him comprehensively as part of all those at different points, that's yet a different kind of relationship. In America, we primarily deal with God as Judge. So therefore, I've got to get it right. I've got to accomplish some things and get it right because I don't want to be wrong.

Another major consideration is whether I see God as more holy or more loving. I see Him as a loving God, but the context of American theology from Anselm and the Reformation on is a judicial God, a legal God, so therefore I'm not interested in a relationship—I want to get this thing right. Tell me what I can do to get this right. That's not a relationship—that's a judgment.

Renée: And then if I don't get it right, I'm in real trouble. I then try to figure out how to get back into good graces with God.

Bishop: And the only thing I know to do is to produce something—to do something right, and then God will love me. You can never pay for nor win God's love. You can receive it as a gift, but you can't win it.

Renée: Which goes back to the basics we're taught about God's love.

Bishop: Back to the basics. The reason we're in trouble is not because of a couple of pieces that are not in place, but the entire prototype is built on a perspective of God that just keeps building the wall higher and higher.

Renée: Then we get locked behind that wall, and get stuck, and can't understand why we're so miserable in our relationship with God.

Bishop: And then what happens is when I start to try to talk to people about it, they don't know what I'm talking about so therefore, I'll be quiet and just work in quiet desperation.

Renée: Which is where I'm seeing a trend, especially in some younger people who seem to be disillusioned with the church. They are trying to go it alone or with a few people who are also disillusioned and trying to work this thing out, but getting more and more stuck, in a sense.

Bishop: It could be that they are caught up in the details. It's not the details that are important; it's where those details point that is important. That all goes back to how you see God. If you see God as a detailed God who is giving you these details to keep, then that's where you'll get stuck. If you see Him as a Father who is trying to help you grow, then that will create a whole different pattern for you. That's the same perspective with pastors and with churches, that how I see God orchestrates what kind of relationship I have with Him. I want to please God, so how do I best please Him? The answer may not match the answer of most church people. The way that I please God is by loving Him and by being in an intimate relationship with Him, not by doing some legal thing. Some people, then, are stuck because all of America is on a legalistic plane. Justice in America has been infused with the idea of a debt and somebody must pay the debt. Whereas justice is overcome by the free gift of God, which is grace and favor. It is not because Jesus paid something for me. That's where we stop. There may be some sense of a debt, but if Jesus paid for me and legally got me free of a debt, that's not love, that's payment. His love far exceeds payment, and His love is not based on payment, even though it paid a debt. His love is that I love you so much that I give my life for you. That's no debt; that's favor. We need to start treating God as a loving father, rather than a legal judge.

PART 2 - PROCESSING PAIN FOR EMOTIONAL HEALTH

GRIEF AND LOSS—THE DARK PLACE

Renée: In one of my grief recovery support groups, we talked about the dark place of grief. There was a parent whose child died. The person said, "I'm not ready to leave the darkness because that's where I meet my child."

Bishop: That's powerful. It's in the dark places that God resides. But we are typically afraid of the darkness and we do everything we can to flee from it.

But the dark night of the soul is where God manifests Himself.

"Weeping may last through the night, but joy comes with the morning" (Psalm 30:5b, NLT).

Renée: In your book, *Grief—A Biblical Pathway to God*, on page 57, you said, "Being made in the likeness in the image of God, we too must do our grief work or repent deeply if we want to be healthy." Explain that.

Bishop: One thing we don't do is we don't see God as grieving. The early church fathers taught that God was impassive, that He had no emotion, because they were trying to protect Him from sin. The Bible says we are made in His likeness, and it is clear in many verses that God the Father, God the Son, and God the Holy Spirit grieves. The Bible is full of instances of grief and loss.

- Ecclesiastes 3:4 implicitly says that there is "a time to cry and a time to laugh. A time to *grieve* and a time dance."
- Genesis 6:6—"And it repented the LORD that he had made man on the earth, and it *grieved* him at his heart."
- Isaiah 53:3-4—"He is despised and rejected by man, A Man of sorrows and acquainted with *grief,* And we hid, as it were, our faces from Him; He was despised, and we did not esteem Him. Surely He has borne our *griefs* and carried our sorrows; Yet we esteemed Him stricken, smitten by God and afflicted."
- Isaiah 53:10—"But the LORD was pleased to crush Him, putting Him to *grief.*"
- Ephesians 4:30—"And do not *grieve* the Holy Spirit of God, by whom you were sealed for the day of redemption."
- Hebrews 4:15-16—"This High Priest of ours understands our weaknesses, for he faced all of the same testings we do, yet he did not sin. So let us come boldly to the throne of our gracious God. There we will receive his mercy, and we will find grace to help us when we need it most."

Note from Renée: For a more comprehensive and exhaustive study of the Biblical concept of grief, consider reading *Grief—A Biblical Pathway to God* and *The God Who Grieves* by Bishop Joey Johnson.

We need a way of processing deep emotions.

Emotions - You can either deal with them or they will deal with you.

THE CASE FOR THE GRIEF RECOVERY METHOD® (GRM)

Renée: Please elaborate on processing the pain, particularly of grief and loss, and any pain that people hold on to, sometimes for years. I've heard you say that when we don't deal with the pain, it comes out sideways.

Bishop: Unless we work with the pain of grief and bring it up, it comes out sideways. An analogy we use when we go to the Grief Recovery Method certification training is when you have pain and you act like a cat. When a cat does personal grooming, it gets hair down in its stomach. When it gets down in there, unless it comes up and out, it will make the cat sick and may kill it. We have a tendency to swallow our pain, take it down inside of us—it wallows around and does whatever it does, and that's why it comes out sideways. It will make us sick because we're not processing it, we're not dealing with it—it's just rolling around. Another analogy is our body is designed to process certain kinds of fat. There are other kinds of fat our body doesn't know what to do with, or is not prepared to process or handle it. So it just goes down and globules in our body. God has given us certain ways to process pain, but in America, because we're so intellectual and rational, we try to process pain through rationality, and it won't work. You can't rationalize your way out of pain; you have to feel some of the things that are going on. Just as when you're in a dark room in your house, you have to feel your way. Even though the lights are out, you know approximately where you are in the room, so you begin to feel your way to the other side of the room. When you have pain, you have to feel your way to the other side. You can't think your way to the other side. Processing is more feeling them and feeling them appropriately, rather than repressing or suppressing them and all the things we do to push them down.

We don't recognize that pain is energy that is seeking to come back up. When you take a bubble bath, you can push one bubble with your hand or wrist, but there are not enough body parts to hold all the bubbles down. When we keep swallowing pain over the course of our lives, after a while, there's not enough to keep it down, and it will come up and out, but it doesn't come out straight. If you process it, it comes out straight. If we don't process it properly, it comes out sideways. It comes out in anger, in frustration, in depression, unhealthy habits, sin, substance abuse, etc. It comes out in all kinds of ways because it is energy that is seeking to be released.

One of the ways God has given us to release it is through tears. The chemical makeup of grief tears is different from the chemical makeup of normal tears. God has created us to cry. What I've learned over a lot of study and time is that crying is not a rational perspective; you don't have to learn how to cry. It's built in from the beginning for you to express something so that your parents can read and understand there is a need. It's pre-rational and pre-verbal. But we've learned in America to suppress our tears, and therefore it's not acting as an escape valve. When I do Grief Recovery Workshops, I carry a steam kettle with a red cork in the spout. Then I ask what will happen when I put water in it and heat it up. They answer, "an explosion!" So if you keep pushing things inside of you and won't release it, an explosion will happen. It could be a moral explosion, a psychological explosion, or anything, but it will explode. Processing pain means that I am probably crying; I am feeling; I am talking about it, and I'm working my way through it. What Americans do is put it away. Americans will repress it or suppress it.

Renée: Is there a difference?

Bishop: To suppress means I'm doing it voluntarily or intentionally. To repress, there are unconscious mechanisms that are taking place. So whether I'm suppressing or repressing, I'm not dealing with the pain, and it's just simply sitting inside of me doing crazy stuff.

Renée: How do you get pastors, churches, church folk, and anyone to process the pain of grief and do something about it?

Bishop: Grief Recovery Method™ Workshops are so import-ant because the method itself deals with processing the pain. When people ask why it's so important for me to go through the Grief Recovery Method Workshop, I tell them because you're not processing the pain, the *energy of grief.* I tell people you can handle your pain or it can handle you.

Grief is the most off limit topic in the Western speaking world. People don't know what grief is; they don't know they need to grieve, and then they ask, "What's wrong with me?"

You can handle your pain or it can handle you.

I do introductory workshops that explain grief itself—why they need it, and then point them to the method of grief re-covery workshops. After some of the workshops, pastors have had their leaders certified as grief recovery specialists or they will go through the workshops. At my church, grief recovery is a pre-requisite for ministry because you're not going to put your sicknesses all over people. If you don't go through grief recovery, you will not be approved for ministry. You need to grieve. So when someone comes and they tell me that they have prayed and the Lord has delivered them from their grief, I tell them, *"No, don't spiritualize your grief. You can't spiri-tualize away the pain you're in.* You're going to have to work through this." These are normal, naturally built in mecha-nisms that God has given you to work through this, and you can't pray this away.

Renée: You have said that some of the reasons pain is not processed is because of lack of training or mentorship.

Bishop: Our culture does not deal well with pain. "Never let them see you sweat." "Just don't deal with it." "Put it away." "Let's move forward." "Stop bringing it up." "Let bygones be bygones."

Renée: Amplify a little more about your book, *Family Mess,* and how it corroborates with processing not only the pain of grief and loss, but any emotional pain. In the instance of a loved one who dies, after the funeral, we usually put that mask back on. We'll cradle our grief for a moment and then tuck it away, adding it to the stockpile of unresolved or incomplete feelings of pain because, we're "too blessed to be stressed."

Bishop: The Scripture that I use as a foundation in the book is the sins of the parents are passed down to the third and fourth generation. In actuality, when you study it, it doesn't mean the sins of the parents, but the *consequences* of their sins or family sin that impacts generation after generation.

THE FOLLOWING IS A QUOTE FROM BISHOP JOHNSON'S BOOK, *FAMILY MESS*:

"When we say something is a mess, we mean that the situation is disorderly, confusing, muddled, troubling, difficult, untidy, dirty, and thus embarrassing. Disorder means a lack of normal order, suggesting an upset of the normal functions or health of something. Consequently, "mess" is strongly related to the concept of dysfunctionality. Family sin leads to family dysfunction: It's a family mess!"

"Families in a mess have three rules that every member usually follows:

- Don't talk.
- Don't feel.
- Don't trust.

"Family mess is a part of life. It's not something you can avoid, but it is something you can heal from. The Bible is a real book that gives the real story of real people and their real interaction with the real God! Therefore the Bible is full of family mess. God does not hide that truth! He deals with reality. There can be no healing or freedom from family mess until we face the reality of what has happened." (pp. 19-20)

Bishop: There is also a great book I've read from the Minirth-Meier Clinic Series, *Kids Who Carry Our Pain*. It deals with whatever you struggle with and don't finish, your children will finish. If you have problems with money, it will come out in your children somewhere. If you have problems with adultery somewhere, it will come out in your children. They will finish what you don't finish. When we see pain passed down to the third and fourth generation, we're talking about something that needs to be handled or grieved.

Renée: Elaborate more on the dynamics of generational behaviors. You used a term, "home of origin" and that we don't understand these issues that can go into the constellation of things that keep us from processing pain. What do you mean by "home of origin"? How do I successfully handle that in a way that leads to emotional and holistic health?

Bishop: What you have going on is "family system disease." It's not something that you are doing as an individual; it's something that has been programmed in you from your home of origin. Even though you are unaware of it, there are some things you have learned that are down in you from before you were even conscious and are setting the context for the things you believe; what you feel; what you know; what you believe is right; what you value...it's all there. You are carrying something of your family. The book, *Kids Who Carry Our Pain*, deals with that. Your pain is not a discreet part of pain that is by itself; it's part of a system of the family you grew up in. It's impacted all of you and everybody in your family, although they respond differently. All relationships are unique and all people are unique, and they respond differently. If a traumatic thing happens in a home, everybody is impacted whether they know it or not. So that impact needs to be dealt with and needs to be factored in.

That's why the grief recovery method works so well because of the tools learned to process pain in relationships. That's another thing people don't want to do. For example, one may say, "I got fired." No, you didn't get fired, somebody fired you. There's a relationship there. Who you are comes out of relationships you have. The impact of what you consider to be yourself, comes out of relationships you have, so relationships become highly important.

We think we make relationships, but actually relationships make us. If it were not for our parents, we would not be here. We learn from them; we are like sponges; we absorb so many things from them. So the "home of origin" becomes the context in which I want to explore what happened to me. Why do I feel like I feel? Why are there certain painful things in my life? What is the root of those things? So when I begin to process them, I'm processing that pain. The good thing about the grief recovery process is it's already set up to process the pain in relationships. We teach that you don't have to forgive each person in your life or try to forgive yourself, that when you begin to release people through the GRM process, you will end up releasing those people in your home of origin and forgiving them and setting them free. It will set you free. We're processing that pain. There are certain tools we use, the Loss History Graph and the Relationship Graph. We use them both as tools, thus processing those "home of origin" issues.

Renée: I've worked with someone who has significant losses in a short span of time. As the family was cleaning out personal items, they found papers and other things that were not known. It helped to put things in a proper perspective.

Bishop: In actuality, not only were family truths and relationships discovered, self-discovery was happening, which can be very liberating. This can aid in processing the pain.

When we start losing relationships, we start losing who we are and get to the real you. Relationships are the basis of our identity. We can begin to understand and embrace our home of origin. This becomes so important so we can process what's going on and what has happened to us in our homes of origin. For some people, it has stunted them or scarred them for the rest of their life. For others, it sets them up for a healthier rest of their life.

Renée: So the way to get people in general, especially church folk, to see the need to do the grief work or process the pain, any pain, is what?

Bishop: To get church people to accept this, we have to artificially "biblicize" it, since the GRM is not a church or Bible program. If you don't biblicize, then they won't take it because they want to see it in the Bible. That's why I wrote the book, *Grief—A pathway to God* to give a biblical context and a grid to the method so you can see it is not anti-biblical. Actually, it is very biblical. But everything you need to deal with does not need to be proof texted. Another problem is the church does not want to deal with any kind of pain or anything to do with psychology. We have an allergy to psychology because of rationalism; we think it is going to attempt to undermine the Bible and therefore don't want to be a part of it. We don't think there is any psychology in the Bible, but the word in the original Greek text translated to "soul" in English is the word "psyche." In Greek, it is spelled "psuche." "Psyche" means the same as "soul."

The Bible is all about psychology, not American psychology, but Hebrew psychology. We are trying to put together several workshops in the city of Akron, Ohio, for pastors to come together to talk about the process of pain. To understand why they don't want to deal with their pain, why you won't help your people deal with their pain, what's blocking you—because there is a major blockage that keeps church people from going down and dealing with this. The thought is "I've got Jesus, and that's enough." That's not enough. If you look at the psychology of the Bible and look at what He does,

He sometimes doesn't automatically heal people. Look at the woman at the well. Jesus had an interview with her where he diagnosed her problem—offered her help.

THE PROCESS OF FORGIVENESS

I look at the GRM as "deep forgiveness" or the process of forgiveness, which we do not have in the church. That's another problem. We will exhort you toward forgiveness, but there is no method of how to do it. There is an action of forgiveness (the Bible says to forgive); there is an attitude (Jesus said to always be ready to forgive); but there has to be a process of forgiveness when I'm dealing with deep pain, which cannot be dismissed in a simple action, event, or act. GRM is that process where I deal with the pain. If you've been abused by somebody, you cannot simply forgive them. You have to work through that pain.

Renée: And it hurts.

Bishop: Yes, it hurts, and you can't do it quickly. It takes time. The process allows me to forgive them. I tell church people, the very actions of the GRM program are found in the Bible, forgiveness, amends, significant emotional stuff... that's all Bible. It's just the Bible stuff we don't practice.

Renée: It requires work. A lot of times, we read the Bible and don't factor in the time that it took for Jesus to do what He did. We read it as instantaneous act.

Bishop: We look for supernatural, miraculous. Jesus is going to do it. Sometimes I run into people who have a smoking problem. They want God to take the taste of cigarettes out of their mouth. We know God can do anything, and for some people He may have done it. But for many people, they've got to break the habit through the power of the Holy Ghost.

Now we're talking about theology—you have an event, but you also have process. What we often end up talking about is simply the act, the event, and not dealing with the process. I call it crisis and process. When you get saved, you have a crisis (you accepted Jesus Christ), and then starts the process of sanctification. So with pain, you get the counseling. We pray for you, and now you've got the process.

THE GRIEF OF SUICIDE

Renée: Let's talk about an issue that seems to be prevalent today. We've had celebrities who have committed suicide. And then we have instances in the church. There's a story of a young pastor with a wife and children who took them to church and then went back home and killed himself. Just recently, I read an article of a pastor with a wife and several young children and a thriving church who took his own life. The pastor in the picture shown with his family was "all smiles." In the church, how do we handle this often forbidden topic or misunderstood act?

Bishop: It happens in the church, and then sometimes we end up doing the funeral. At my church, we process and handle funerals very well. Remember, all members of my staff are certified grief recovery specialists, and my leadership team have all gone through the grief recovery method workshops. We do funerals from a different perspective, including when the death is by suicide.

It's a wonder there are not more suicides in America with the angst, the hopelessness, the confusion of American life. The government, the President, the White House are not helping. They're making it more chaotic. We seem to be going backwards instead of forward—backwards in civility, backwards in honesty, backwards in diversity. That adds anxiety. I read a book called *Post Traumatic Slave Syndrome*. It deals with the fact that as an African American person living in a society where you constantly have to be on guard, this will create a post-traumatic stress response in your life. Could it be that African Americans' blood pressure is higher than whites not simply because it is physiological, but because it is sociological and psychological that we have to constantly be on guard? We don't know what is going to happen in this society, and therefore has raised our blood pressure physiologically of our entire race. With that kind of angst, pain, chaos, people just feel hopeless. And then in the African American community, the church used to be the main resource. So even if I'm hopeless, I go to a place where there is hope. We no longer have that. I may not go to church, or I may not have those resources there if I do go. I'm being pumped full of anxiety by watching the TV and the news. Feeling hopeless and have no guardrails, no boundaries that say if I take my life, what will be the ultimate impact? I'm not saved—I don't have a society that helps me with that anymore. So if I take my life, that's just it. I'm just gone. There's no sense of where I will spend eternity; what will happen? So people are taking their lives on a more frequent basis because society has changed. Now how do we handle that? First, we have to deal with church people, and what do we believe about people who have committed suicide?

Renée: Right, do we believe that is the one unpardonable sin?

Bishop: Many people believe that. I don't believe it is. If salvation is a gift—I didn't do anything to get it, I can't do anything to lose it. So therefore, suicide wouldn't be the thing that causes me to lose my salvation. One of my friends used to say that when you commit suicide, you enter into the presence of God unannounced! God looks up and says, "What are you doing here?"

So the problem is not that you committed suicide, but that you entered God's presence unannounced! Maybe that wasn't supposed to be your time. The problem also is that those who commit suicide are committing the ultimate selfish act. They're not considering what it's going to do to those left behind. The folks who are left behind are ruined because they're constantly asking themselves, "Why didn't I see what was going on? I should have done this or that." That's problematic to the nth degree because they're trapped in something that is difficult to get them out of.

Second, how do I help the family? I don't help the family in the expected way because I'm not caught in church tradition. I tell them that their loved one's choice, as devastating as it was, it was their choice. You can't change their choice; you can't bring them back. As painful as it is, the thing you can do is to accept their choice. Since you can't change it, why don't you accept it? They insist they should have seen it. I tell them there is no way you could have seen it. They are very good at hiding it. There's nothing you could have done.

Third, at the funeral, I deal with some of the myths of death. One Christian myth is that "God was getting lonely. He went down and got the best flower out the garden." I don't believe that God sits in heaven and arbitrarily chooses people to die. I've had people get mad because I don't preach what they want. Then they will say to me, "Well the Bible says, that 'it's appointed once for every man to die and after that the judgment.'" Then I will say, "If you look it up in any translation, what it means is that every person on earth must die and then be judged." It doesn't mean that for every person God chooses an arbitrary appointment or a day for them to die. It's a combination of things—choice, other people's choices, a combination of what they did, where they lived, what they ate, drank, etc. There are a whole lot of reasons as to why they die. But God did not sit up in heaven and "take" them. If you teach that, you will ruin your children. They will wake up one day and say, "God took my Daddy." And then you think they'll come to God for a relationship with Him? Children don't have the rational ability to even understand what you mean by that. So I try to help them understand that God didn't take your loved one. In fact, Jesus said, "Lo, I'm with you always." He cares about you. He's sitting "shiva" with you. *("sitting shiva," is to create an environment of comfort and community for mourners: It helps guide friends and family members through the loss of a loved one.)* If you read in the second New Living Translation, God says, "The Lord cares deeply when His loved ones die" (Psalm 116:15) and God grieves when they die.

So then they ask why would God grieve if He's taken somebody, and why would He grieve if He's God and He could have prevented it? He grieves because we have choices, and He allows those choices. He grieves because He loves us, and He knows the impact of our death. He grieves because He can't depend upon us anymore on earth to do certain things and have certain interactions. He grieves because our families are torn apart. There are a lot of reasons why God grieves. So with regard to suicide, therefore, I can help the family deal with your child, your spouse, your loved one's choice. It's a devastating choice, but if you can accept that, then you can trust Jesus and He'll walk with you through anything and will help you. I ask, "Do you believe your loved one would want you to be sitting here torn up? What do you think he'd want you to do? If you think he'd want you to go on, then we'll work on that."

Suicide can be one of the most devastating things someone could do because you always ask at some point, "Why didn't I see it? Why couldn't I stop it?" And underneath it is a little bit of a feeling, "I wonder if I did something to cause it?" So we must prepare ourselves to deal better with the event of suicide.

Renée: How would you speak to the followers of those pastors and other influential leaders who took their lives? We assume the pastors were saved. They preached about the love of God.

Bishop: I start with making sure we understand that no act that anyone can do can save them and no act can damn them. So we believe those pastors are saved, and are right now in the presence of the Lord. No more struggles, no more pain, no more issues.

Second, the only people we have to worry about are us. How are we going to process this, and how will we move through this? How shall we get healthy? How can we best honor this person in their death and their life? What do you think they would want us to do? Other than that, you're left with nothing but hopelessness.

Renée: And someone who might be hopeless anyway, and weak since we don't know what people are going through, may say, "Well, pastor did it."

Bishop: Yes, the pastor was the model and some may try to imitate them.

This is the kind of deep stuff we're into with grief work and emotional health, and I pray that God will use your book to touch many people.

Renée: I pray so. I can't begin to thank you enough because you've shared such a wealth of deep information that typically you may not hear on a regular basis. I hope this book will be a stimulus, a catalyst for people to consider.

[END OF CONVERSATION]

Books by Bishop Joey Johnson mentioned in this conversation:

Grief—A Biblical Pathway to God

The God Who Grieves

Family Mess

Suggested readings:

Kids Who Carry Our Pain—Breaking the Cycle of Codependency for the Next Generation by Dr. Robert Hemfelt and Dr. Paul Warren

Post Traumatic Slave Syndrome: America's Legacy of Enduring Injury and Healing by Dr. Joy DeGruy

The Grief Recovery Method Handbook by John W. James and Russell Friedman

Misreading Scripture with Western Eyes—Removing Cultural Blinders to Better Understand the Bible by E. Randolph Richards and Brandon J. O'Brien

Considerations?

_____

_____

_____

_____

_____

_____

Confessions?

_____

_____

_____

_____

_____

Convictions?

_____

_____

_____

_____

_____

More Conversations?

_____

_____

_____

_____

_____

Dirge of Grief

Maybe if I hold my breath and refuse to breathe,
It will unlock me from its grip so I can run away.
They yell at me, "breathe, c'mon now, breathe" as if giving birth,
only this thing is death delivered.
I'd much rather be somewhere else, anywhere else but here.
Even if I escape and run until I'm out of breath, I'll be found.
They say it will have its way with me until it's done.
It masquerades to seem complete, then sorely winks that it's not.
So have your way for now. Run. Sit. Lay down with me.
Make your way to that once forbidden place
where it's dark, dank and quietly loud.
Where other pains of loss slept fitfully undisturbed until now.
I'll follow if I must, trowel in hand for this merciless dig.
Deep into the bowels of my earth, cutting, scooping up what's been waiting.
It's where WHY lives.
I may choose to join them, kick at them, prodding my discovery.
Breathe into them so we can talk.
Stay as long as I want.
When it's time to go, I will ask them to walk up with me
into the light for a breath of fresh air.
And then send them on their way.

CHAPTER 8

SOUL CARE FOR SUBSTANCE ABUSE

Forgiveness—An Open Door to Emotional Health

In Conversation with **Dr. Ramona Joseph, B.S., B.A., M.A.T.S., D.Min.**

DR. RAMONA JOSEPH, affectionately known as Dr. Mom, was born in Chicago, Illinois. She relocated to Charlotte, North Carolina, in 2006; in 2015 relocated to Sumter, South Carolina; and in 2016 to the Dallas-Fort-Worth Metroplex. She served for fifteen years as the organizing senior pastor of a south side Chicago church, GOD NEVER FAILS Healing and Deliverance Ministries. Her undergraduate education was received from Roosevelt and DePaul Universities. She holds a Master of Theological Studies from McCormick Theological Seminary and a Doctor of Ministry from the Chicago Theological Seminary.

Dr. Joseph served as co-host of Chicago's popular *Let's Talk About Marriage and the Family* on Christian radio, WYCA. She was seen weekly for over ten years on the Chicago television production, *Life Changing Experiences.* Dr. Joseph has served as a State of Illinois certified Domestic Violence Counselor and a licensed Pastoral Counselor. In 2006, Dr. Joseph relocated to Charlotte, North Carolina. She served as Executive Administrative pastor of the Greater Salem Church. She continued her educational pursuits and completed two years of training in the Carolinas Healthcare system's Clinical Pastoral Education. In addition, Dr. Joseph served as Academic Dean of the Queen City Bible College. She served as the leader of the ministerial alliance of the Nations Ford Community Church under the leadership of its then pastors, Drs. Phillip M. Davis and Cynthia L. Davis. In 2015, Dr. Joseph served as a staff chaplain at the Palmetto Health—Tuomey Regional Medical Center in Sumter, South Carolina.

Dr. Joseph is a board certified chaplain through the Association of Professional Chaplains. She served as Chair of the Northeast Medical Center of Concord, North Carolina, Chaplaincy Advisory Committee. She served as the Continuing Education Chair of South Carolina Association of Professional Chaplains. Ramona is continuing to fulfill her passion as a professional chaplain-counselor at Valley Hope Association in Grapevine, Texas, a 60-bed, inpatient substance abuse facility.

Dr. Joseph has authored and published a monthly devotional book, *God Never Fails,* during the years 1979-1984. She authored *WOMAN, the Spirituality of God* and *LORD, Teach Us to Pray,* an intercessory prayer training manual. It is Dr. Joseph's plan to complete the final rewrite to publish a self-help book entitled *Stop Tripping Over Your Past.*

Dr. Joseph attends The Potter's House in Fort Worth where her spiritual son and daughter, Patrick Winfield and his wife Lady V. serve as Campus Pastors.

[BEGINNING OF CONVERSATION]

Renée: You have served as pastor, hospital chaplain, teacher, mentor, and now you're chaplain in the area of substance abuse. How has your experience in caring for the souls of your congregation, hospital patients, and their families and countless others helped in caring for those dealing with addictions?

Dr. Ramona Joseph

Dr. Joseph: The greatest pastoral ministry is the one God gives you to facilitate, whether with a congregation of many parishioners or in a chaplain-counseling session with one patient. One thing learned has been a soul (the mind, will, intellect, emotions, or imaginations) of each, whether able to walk into a church building for help or to walk into a rehabilitation treatment center, the needs may differ somewhat, but the foundation is the same. A child of God needs a shepherd.

Renée: Because those you care for may or may not be a believer in the Christian faith, how do you deal with the spiritual implications of substance abuse as a chaplain?

Dr. Joseph: The Twelve-Step Alcoholics or Narcotics program at Valley Hope of Grapevine starts with a licensed, substance counselor helping the patient to admit they are powerless when it comes to their particular substance. This is done with the patient completing an eight-page document concerning their substance abuse, how it started, how it affected their life, etc. The review of step one is done by the substance abuse counselor; it is a thorough review and may take several sessions for the patient to admit they are powerless to their substance. My job as a chaplain-counselor is to take the patient through the next steps, generally in rehab, that would be steps two through eight, which include that the patient admits that a power greater than ourselves could restore us to sanity and then make a decision to turn our will and lives over to the care of God as we understood Him.

Many of our patients have a religious background. However, to work the twelve-step program does not mean you have to be religious, but you must be spiritual. Each patient must have and connect with a Higher Power they feel will help them overcome their substance abuse. If a patient is Atheist or Agnostic, it does not pose a problem because they do believe in something. There are five spiritual powers I try to introduce to my patients that are Atheist or Agnostic as follows: the Universe, Love, Humanity, Music, and Nature. Some will only refer to the Higher Power by those two words, Higher Power. Others will use the acronym we all embrace, whether Christian or not, **G**ood **O**rderly **D**irection. I tell my Atheist or Agnostic patients, prayer is simply a verbal or silent request, wish, or hope, done in the belief it is heard and will be answered. The student in school says when they failed to do their homework, "God, I hope she doesn't call on me today" (another reason prayer will never be taken out of the school systems!). *Whether Christian, Jewish, Buddhist, Atheist, or Agnostic; the key to our profession of faith is that we do not over think or confuse ourselves.*

Renée: What do you do to safeguard your emotional and mental health in dealing with so much emotional, and sometimes mental chaos/darkness in the soul of the substance abuser?

Dr. Joseph: My formula to safeguard my emotional and mental health is prayer. I always wish and hope I will hear what my patients are saying, as well as what they are not saying. I can only do that by depending totally on my Higher Power, The Lord God Jehovah. The Bible says, "He (the Spirit of Truth) will guide you into *ALL* truth" (John 16:13, NKJV). My foolishness will be to get into a place where I am dependent on myself and not Him.

Renée: Do you have a chaplain, counselor, a mentor?

Dr. Joseph: After spending two years in Clinical Pastoral Education (CPE), I learned the benefit of "self-care." Each week, there was one hour spent with the CPE supervisor discussing feelings, your patient caseload, personal issues, and struggles you might be having as a chaplain. So, I know the value of a counselor. Further, as a board-certified chaplain through the Association of Professional Chaplains, each year in January, I must submit my annual report of continuing education. A portion of that report must indicate I have participated in several hours of "self-care." I generally see my counselor every 90 to 120 days. My recent relocation from South Carolina to Texas (November, 2016) was traumatic after discovering I did not have the position I had been promised. For another eight months, I was unemployed. When I started working at Valley Hope of Grapevine, I could hardly wait until I had a counselor termed in corporate America, EAP counselor.

Renée: Emotional wellness is essential to the office of pastor/chaplain because you are the keeper, sometimes the object of a myriad of personalities, emotions, dysfunctions of the souls entrusted to you. With that said, people can be disappointed and blaming when they may not get from you what they want or expect. This could lead to hurtful behavior towards you. As a believer in the tenets of Christ, you're to forgive that person who may have hurt you and deeply offended you. As a human emotional being, your impulsive and natural response might be unforgiveness. How do you safeguard your soul from prolonged unforgiveness?

Dr. Joseph: Unforgiveness is recognized by some physicians as the root cause for autoimmune diseases, arthritis, fibromyalgia, and diseases. The Bible speaks of the root of bitterness (Hebrews 12:15) and the rottenness of the bones (Proverbs 14:30).

I cannot lead my patient through the twelve steps, [Step four—Make a searching and fearless moral inventory of ourselves] stressing forgiveness, and I am unable to forgive. My daily prayer is, "Father, forgive me of those things I have (not may have **but have)** done that caused pain and anguish to someone, as I forgive those that have caused me pain and anguish." Daily, we say and do things, not intentionally, that cause pain and anguish. To sincerely seek forgiveness opens doors to remove any and all unforgiveness.

Renée: I want to talk about unforgiveness more, but before I do, I would be remiss if we didn't talk about the opioid crisis that is at an epidemic level in our society right now. What should the church's response be, and how do we embrace this as "our" problem, or do we?

Dr. Joseph: The opioid crisis is "our" problem. I wonder if the Church is prepared to respond. The temperament of many people is that all you have to do is just quit. The disease is far greater than just stopping because a person goes to rehab. At Valley Hope, patients attend classes, do individual counseling. Some require a psychiatrist to prescribe medication for other disorders; patients learn to talk about themselves and what has transpired in their lives in their respective small groups that are co-ed, and then to talk in their gender groups that are all male or all female. They read about the disease and they attend lectures to help them understand the disease. Nightly, there are Twelve-Step meetings at the facility. Patients must work on their aftercare plan. It is difficult to go through rehab, but then the real work starts when they leave and are in recovery for the entire balance of their lives. Rehab and recovery do not mean "cured." There are many complexities of the substance abuse disease. AA groups and Al-Anon groups host meetings throughout the day at various home groups. And there is much more I could share. Many people are not going to want to be pointed out in a congregation as a recovering alcoholic or a recovering substance abuser. An AA or Al-Anon group would not be embraced as the Marriage Ministry, Men's Ministry, or Singles' Ministry. Support can be given by what a congregation can provide keeping in mind to pursue support for a home group should be consistent and ongoing. For example, if a room in the church is used for meetings, when it is pastoral anniversary time, the room should still be available for the meeting; people that attend meetings are creatures of habit!

Renée: Let's talk about the issue of forgiveness. How does unforgiveness lend itself to emotional and mental instability and negatively affect your soul care?

Dr. Joseph: I see what unforgiveness can do to people. I had a patient tell me, after asking him if he had asked for forgiveness say, "I've told my family repeatedly I am sorry, but I have never said forgive me." He called their names and asked forgiveness for his actions as an alcoholic. Suddenly he started to cry; he kept crying and finally said, "This is the first time I have felt free."

Forgiveness, given and received, creates a freedom that many people will never experience. People will say they have asked God to forgive them, but they cannot forgive themselves. I point people to the 1 John 1:9 Scripture where the writer states that God is faithful and just to forgive us...and cleanse us. When a person cannot forgive themselves, call themselves Christian believers, they are trying to be more than God. Is it any wonder they are not free? A parable I use with my patients is asking them if they shower. The response is, "Yes."

I ask, "Did you shower to cleanse yourself." The response is, "Yes." When you finished cleansing, turned off the water, did you go into the drain and say, "This is what the soap was able to cleanse, but I cannot cleanse myself of this!"? When God forgives, it all goes down the drain. Likewise when we forgive, it should all go down the drain.

Renée: When a patient asks someone for forgiveness and that person refuses to forgive, what do you tell that patient to do so they can still be free?

Dr. Joseph: Sometimes we'll just do forgiveness in my office. I'll say, "Your spouse is not here, your children aren't here, and whoever is not here."

I recall a patient whose father died when he was a toddler and whose mother, though a professional, was morbidly obese. He resented her for being so big. She worked hard every day and they never lacked for anything. I said, "Have you ever asked for her forgiveness? I know she's dead, but you can ask her right now to forgive you. God will hear you and that you have a contrite heart and you're sorry for thinking ill against your mother. God hears you whether your mother can hear it or not. God says that He accepts the fact that you want to seek forgiveness, and he allows you to be free." The patient said to his mother, "Please forgive me for all the times I was ashamed and embarrassed about you." Then he started to call the names of the other kids' mothers who would not invite his mother to their events. He called every one of those ladies by name, and said, "I forgive you Mrs. ___; he called about five people's names because he had harbored such resentment and anger against them because they were all thin and nice looking and his mother was fat."

Renée: We do that in grief recovery as well, when the person is deceased and simply can't talk to them for whatever reason.

Dr. Joseph: I say to that person, stop saying, "I'm sorry." Ask for forgiveness. If the person says, "I can't forgive you," then just leave it, because what happens is God has heard that and God will deal with them if they can't forgive you. God heard your sincerity when you said, "Please forgive me," and He has freed you. In cases like that, there is a breaking—people will sit in my office and call names and say, "Please forgive me." They may cry for ten minutes, and I just let them cry.

When they finish, I'll say to them, "How do you feel?" They will say they feel so free and it feels as if a hundred pounds have been lifted off of them.

Even in the church, there is so much unforgiveness. We may say, "I can forgive but I can't forget." If God says that He's taken sin away from us as far as the east is from the west, then what you're saying is you're trying to be a god, to be bigger or better than God, and that's just not going to work. That's why so many people in church die with all this anger, hostility within themselves, and that is so sad.

Renée: You have given me examples of unforgiveness in your patients. Would you share personal instances where you had to forgive?

FORGIVE MY MOTHER

Dr. Joseph: My mother was never officially diagnosed, but my clinical pastoral education supervisor gave me a book on borderline personality. At that particular time in 2012, it was not even listed as a disorder in the *Diagnostic and Statistical Manual* of Mental Disorders (DSM). It's only been in the last two years that they have listed borderline personality as a disorder. I think I understand now how my mother could be warm one minute and cold the next, how she could not be particularly loving to me but she could be pleasant toward me, but within a matter of minutes, that could change. So I endured a lot of things growing up that were very hurtful. In fact, one time I remember being taken to the doctor, and he wanted to know why I was such a nervous child. But we were not dealing with psychiatry in those days. I tried so desperately to be loved and accepted by my mother. I remember one Christmas, my mother was not working and I had a job and was putting myself through college. I wanted to make Christmas really nice for her because she had been so depressed about not working. She had lost a portion of her eyesight, but it was a miracle that God restored her eyesight.

I had saved my money and bought her a suit and matching blouse and several other things. I wrapped everything so nicely and just thought she'd be so excited to open these Christmas presents. I was trying to bring some joy to her life. I'll never forget when she opened those presents. She cursed me out for everything she could imagine. She said she didn't need this (expletive) thing. She could cuss like a sailor. She threw everything in the floor.

I continued to try to win her. I bought her a brand new car while I rode the bus. I bought her a fur coat. Every winter, I would send my mother to California to visit one of her friends to stay for the whole winter. She didn't know what winter weather was like then. I would give her money.

Over the years, I started to see that some of the ways I was dealing with people was out of anger. It wasn't anger at those people, but it was the anger I had from being so rejected. That was from a place of unforgiveness. I had to continue to work on myself. I realized that other people didn't deserve my anger because I couldn't forgive my mother.

I'll never forget...My mother had her 100th birthday on April 30, 2010. I was living in Charlotte. I went to Chicago and gave my mother a red carpet event. People came from Charlotte, Georgia, and from all over for the celebration. There was a limousine and interviews on the red carpet. My mother was excited and very happy. I know that she really enjoyed herself. A lot of prominent Chicago ministers were there. We had the Lord's Supper, a beautiful meal, and decorated the room with her favorite colors of purple and red.

Shortly after that, my mother experienced a fall. Later the doctors discovered a cervical fracture at the base of her skull not associated with the fall, but due to jerking her neck while nodding off to sleep. Coupled with the effects associated with old age, it was recommended she be moved from assisted living to a skilled nursing facility. I went to Chicago to move her, and made sure my mother would receive the best of care. I had friends and former church family members in Chicago to check on her. Someone was there constantly to visit and check on her, to comb her hair, to bring her food, to keep her company. I was flying back and forth to Chicago monthly.

I would call my mother every day from October until Thanksgiving Day. The assistants would place the phone to her ear, but she would not talk to me. I could hear my mother breathing, but she wouldn't respond. I had psychiatric care for her, but they said there was nothing wrong. At that point, I wasn't angry. I just wanted to make sure she had everything that was best for her.

The skilled care facility personnel told me it was then best that she have hospice care. I continued to call every day, and still she wouldn't talk to me on the phone. It was very, very painful, but I said at that particular time I could not allow the pain to burden me down. In my home, I had loads of pictures on my piano of my mother. Looking at those pictures and knowing she was alive and wouldn't talk to me, I had to take them down. I asked God to let me have the peace of forgiveness. Let me forgive her.

On Thanksgiving Day, the members and deacons of my former congregation in Chicago took her Thanksgiving dinner. She asked one of the deacons to call me. When he called, she asked me, "Is everything all right?" I said, "Everything is fine." She then said, "Is everything all right between us?" I insisted, "I said everything is fine." I meant it because it was fine. How was I going to harbor unforgiveness? I had done everything I could for my mother. I'm not going to let unforgiveness rob me of the joy I had for being able to do the things that I could do. I said to her that it may be a little difficult for you to talk to me so

I'm going to start to write you a letter every single day and put it in the mail, and then you'll be able to read letters. I asked the staff to make certain that she had a letter from me every day. She died on December 17.

The only regret I have is not having the experience of a loving mother, especially when I hear people talk about the loving relationship they have or had with their mothers. I saw her being loving and kind to other people. When I look at it, it would be wrong to hold unforgiveness, especially for someone with a mental illness she suffered with. She didn't know it, and I didn't know it then, but she did have a mental illness. She was mentally ill and possibly could not help herself.

FORGIVE MY HUSBAND

My husband promised he would take care of me when I started the church in Chicago because I was traveling so much working for Federal Reserve. He said not to worry because you also have to work full time at the church. However, the things he did against me were very agonizing. He left me with virtually nothing. Right before he died, the last conversation I had with him was as his pastor. I told him I wanted him to recommit himself to God and get right with God and be a Christian. While I didn't go to the funeral, my stepmother went to view the body and I was able to get the program. I was able to see him that year at Easter; he did join the church and recommit his life to Christ.

There were times when I wished I'd had a happy marriage and not been in the position I'm in where I have to work and have no retirement benefits. I wish I could have been the wife "until death do us part." But when I get angry and think about those things, I have to say, "God forgive me for having those thoughts," because God has taken care of me well.

Renée: How long did it take you to get to that place? Is it a gradual realization?

Dr. Joseph: A year or so after Mr. Joseph divorced me, I had a disturbing dream that awakened me at around 2:00 a.m. I'm not a dreamer, but I dreamed Mr. Joseph was in a solid white room and he was just screaming at the top of his lungs. He was trying to climb the wall, screaming and screaming. I got out of my bed and in my spirit, I knew he was sick. I got on my knees and said, "Whatever is wrong with Phillip, if it's about me, don't let him be sick because of me." God said, "It isn't about you." Until the day he died, I sincerely prayed for him. During that week, my ex-sister-in-law called me. She said that Phillip was in a life or death situation. He was in the hospital and we didn't know if he would live or not. It's never been hard for me to forgive people. I told her I knew he was sick and that something was wrong. I then told her about the dream and what God told me when I prayed.

There are times when I think about having to get up at 5:00 a.m. every morning to go to work. I say to God that if I had been better prepared in my life, I wouldn't have to do this. If I started to get angry, it would affect my patients.

The other night, I turned on the television and *The Lion King* was on. It was so unusual because it was right at my favorite part when the lion looks at the monkey and says that he has to go back and deal with his past. He was afraid and didn't want to deal with what happened before.

The little monkey looked at the lion and said, "It's in the past" *(with an accent)*. "You can either run from it or learn from it."

FORGIVE MY LEADER

As a leader in a church ministry, I had endeavored to support the senior leadership in as many ways as I could. The senior leader had shared during the Bible study a family issue that was relative to the sudden death of his parent. It happened to be during the time when the pastor and people in attendance at Bible study were killed in Charleston, South Carolina. The following morning, I sent an email to the members of the group I led; the email was to only twenty plus people in the group, and not a broadcast to the entire church or beyond the church. The email asked for prayers for those that had lost their lives in the Bible study, their family members, some of which belonged to the church I attended. The email further asked for prayers for the senior leader of the congregation that had shared about the failing health of his parent. Within the hour, I received one of the most hurtful email messages from the senior leader. There were no thanks for the prayers; there was nothing positive in the email. It was extremely hurtful to me, as it ripped apart my leadership of the group in the church and tore at my compassion for those murdered, as well as for him and his family. My immediate reaction was to respond, but I was too hurt to be angry. The week passed, and I asked God to forgive me if my actions were wrong, as well as to forgive me for the anger I had for the senior leader. I felt forgiven, and the issue was behind me.

That Saturday, I was in the store at the checkout line. I saw a gift card, and the Holy Spirit reminded me the next day was Father's Day, and I had sent an email to the members of the group I led asking them to remember the senior leader, the spiritual father over us. I looked at the gift card and thought if the Holy Spirit wanted the leader to have a Father's Day gift, it should be given by anyone but me. Then I remembered, first, I was created in the image and likeness of God and it would be me through whom the Father's Day gift would have to be given. Second, I could not lead those under me if I was not prepared to walk a righteous road in front of them. I purchased the gift card. The next day following the worship experience, I stood in the line as others were shaking the senior leader's hand. I got to the front of the line and someone approached him from another side; he responded to them. And then there was another person until finally I was the last person standing in front of him. All the while this was happening, the little monkey was saying, "It's in the past." Finally, I handed him the card and said, "I just wanted to wish you a happy Father's Day." His response was one of shock and he fumbled to say thank you. I walked away from that entire incident FREE.

I'm not saying you're not going to think about the hurtful things that have happened to you, but just look over your shoulder—you can look that far back and say, "It's in the past."

Renée: And now I'm going to have to go back and look at *The Lion King*!

Dr. Joseph: So for me, I can think about it, I can wish what happened had been different, but you know what, "It's in the past." Holding on to unforgiveness keeps you tied up, keeps you angry. I want to be free.

Renée: Finally, I'd like to hear your definition of a healthy soul care provider.

Dr. Joseph: I really do not have a definition of a healthy soul care provider. There are many areas where soul care providers can be found: the bishops and pastors of congregations, the supporting ministerial staff in a church, clinical chaplains in medical centers, hospice centers, substance abuse centers, chaplains in the penal system, in large airports, mental institutions, college campuses, and even more. Each of these soul care providers, while connected as Christians, Jews, and Catholics, meet those of other traditions—Muslims, Buddhists, and more, share a great responsibility to those they are charged to lead.

Parker Palmer in his book, *Let Your Life Speak,* speaks about vocation. "Vocation does not mean a goal that I pursue. It means a calling that I hear. Before I can tell my life what I want to do with it, I must listen to my life telling me who I am."

The more we know who we are, the more we will know how to be healthy, first for ourselves and then for others we serve.

Renée: Thank you, Dr. Joseph. You have been so giving to share out of the depths of your heart some painful things. I appreciate your candor and your transparency.

[END OF CONVERSATION]

Considerations?

_____
_____
_____
_____
_____

Confessions?

_____
_____
_____
_____
_____

Convictions?

_____
_____
_____
_____
_____

More Conversations?

_____
_____
_____
_____
_____

"A spiritually rooted disease is a result of separation from God, separation from yourself and separation from others. The beginning of all healing of spiritually rooted diseases is:
• Reconciliation with God and His Love, receiving His Love, reconciliation with Him as your Father, and making your peace with Him;
• Reconciliation of you with yourself; and
• Reconciliation with others."

—*A More Excellent Way—Be In Health* by Dr. Henry W. Wright
(pp. 216-217)

"A sound heart is the life of the flesh: but envy the rottenness of the bones" (Proverbs 14:30).

"A merry heart doeth good like a medicine: but a broken spirit drieth the bones" (Proverbs 17:22).

"There is no fear in love; but perfect love casts out fear: because fear has torment. He that fears is not made perfect in love" (1 John 4:18).

CHAPTER 9

ALL OF ME—BODY, MIND, SPIRIT

In Conversation with **Dr. Rob and Dr. Karla Robinson**

KINGDOM-DRIVEN husband and wife team, Dr. Robert C. Robinson III, M.D., and Dr. Karla L. Robinson, M.D., have taken an unprecedented multidimensional approach to empowering the community to live their best and healthiest lives yet. Committed to tackling health disparities and improving health literacy and awareness, Drs. Robinson want everyone to experience abundant living.

Knowing what it means to face and conquer health challenges on both a personal and professional level, together they have witnessed the power of God transform lives—allowing many to reclaim their health after living in sickness for years. Recognizing the need to empower the community to become more proactive in maintaining their health, Dr. Karla and Dr. Rob established the Urban Housecall Health Media Group, a comprehensive, multimedia health and wellness resource designed to bring you information on health, healing, and abundant living. Whether through community education, health fairs, public speaking, or personal and corporate consulting, Drs. Robinson are committed to educating you about health maintenance, disease management and prevention, and the risks of neglecting your physical, mental, emotional, and spiritual health.

Dr. Karla Robinson has clinical experience as a board-certified family physician, while Dr. Robert Robinson is a board-certified internal medicine and hospitalist physician. Their combined inpatient and outpatient medicine experience give them the unique ability to service the community as experts on all the health issues that matter to you the most. Both natives of Chicago and alums of Xavier University of Louisiana, Dr. Robert Robinson went on to complete medical school and Internal Medicine Residency training at the University of Illinois at Chicago, while Dr. Karla Robinson completed medical school at Rush University Medical College and Family Medicine Residency Training at Advocate Illinois Masonic Medical Center.

They now reside in Charlotte, North Carolina, where they are active in ministry and are raising their four children.

"Beloved, I pray that you may prosper in all things and be in health, just as your soul prospers" (3 John 2).

Renée: Tell us about the vision, mission, and purpose of Urban Housecall.

Dr. Karla: Urban Housecall is a comprehensive, multi-media health and wellness resource that is designed to bring information on health, healing, and abundant living. Our goal is to provide practical tools that anyone can use to achieve reclaim or maintain their health using biblical principles, nutrition, and healthy lifestyle. We are committed to empower everyone to walk in divine health, even if it's one person at a time. We carry out that vision in a number of ways. Urban Housecall has evolved over the last eight years and continues to evolve. We're in awe at what God has already done, but know that there are so many more layers to be exposed as we continue to seek out our vision.

Dr. Rob & Dr. Karla Robinson

Renée: What are some of the vehicles that you use to get this valuable information out to those who need it the most?

Dr. Rob: As Dr. Karla mentioned, Urban Housecall was actually birthed as an online wellness magazine and has since evolved. It has so many layers to where we're doing television and radio spots; conferences with church organizations; and personal consulting to address the spiritual, physical, emotional, and mental needs on those who call upon us to help them through the challenges they're facing. It is a multidimensional and multi-media vehicle that we use. We're not eliminating any vehicle. We use and operate in every space where God intends to use us to empower God's people to take claim to the divine health. It is not only available, but is truly His mandate for our lives.

Renée: You do a lot of speaking in various venues, and one of those is churches. I want to zero in on that. How receptive are churches to what you have to say about divine health, which is holistic health, spirit, soul, and body? Can I say that sometimes this is a challenge with the church to pay attention to all three parts of us for the sake of balance?

Dr. Karla: I think you hit the nail on the head with that. As a church, we can be so focused on spiritual health that we neglect our physical and emotional health. We understand, as you said, we are a three part or triune being, spirit, soul, and body. We are interconnected; we can't separate the three. If one area is unhealthy, so the other areas will suffer. I love how 3 John 1:2 reminds us that we ought not to just strive for spiritual health but also physical health. We should be healthy physically as we strive to be spiritually. I agree that it is sometimes a challenge to zero in on the fact that all are equally as important. That's why our ministry is so important and seeks to fill that gap to bring to people's remembrance that it's all important. You can't be healthy enough to do God's work if one area is suffering and unhealthy.

Dr. Rob: What has helped us in crossing that divide that might seem like an obstacle in delivering our message of health and wellness to the church is we identify and point out the interconnectivity of spirit, soul, and body. We point out that many of the physical ailments people are dealing with or facing are truly rooted in spiritual causes. Because we come with that understanding and insight, that allows us to enter into some conversations or places that otherwise meet resistance as it relates to addressing physical health. We show how that link is so powerful to identify the root cause, which comes back to what the church should be doing in addressing the spirituality piece.

Renée: There seems to be an escalation of violence, killings, and mass shootings in schools and other public places—hate crimes, substance abuse, sexual assault, bullying, suicide, etc. in these days and times. As the stories unfold, emotional and mental disease too often is a part of the reporting. What would you say specifically to the church when you address the spiritual implications as you've described? Can you leave that church with practical application or actions to take in addressing these issues?

Dr. Rob: We're truly of the belief that every resource that God's people need is truly in the House of God. As it relates to resources, it's actually tapping into those mental health professionals and other health care clinicians in the congregation who are not being utilized. Use the skills and knowledge of those doctors, nurses, counselors, dieticians, health and wellness trainers, etc., who have the understanding but are not being utilized to bring the awareness to and uncover some of the underlying issues that are at the root of the health issues some of the congregants are facing. Just exposing how everything that's needed is in the House is a start. Just tapping into and taking advantage of what's already available, also taking advantage of the power, authority, and dominion that we all have as believers, to fight the principalities in the nation and in our communities. Understanding and operating in the power of our prayer, the words we speak, and the declarations of what God has already proclaimed is paramount. We must empower ourselves with what we have and truly understand what we can do to fight against the spirits and principalities of darkness that we are facing.

Dr. Karla: Again, it takes a multi-dimensional approach. As the church is more powerful than we realize, our approach should be, "Let's have the altar open and then after the altar is closed, on Monday we have to have our wellness center open to get counseling and life skills to walk out this deliverance with behavioral and a lifestyle change." Sometimes we forget to connect the dots, so to speak. We'll attack it from one angle, but then the enemy has place to set up residence again and we haven't experienced true deliverance. So just knowing that we need to cover God's people through every area and like Dr. Rob said, it's all in the House of God, the church, the body of believers. We have what we need to keep ourselves healthy—tapping into that and knowing our power and taking up residence as the warriors that we are. We also are forgetting our place as prayer warriors. We have a responsibility to pray for our leaders, our lawmakers, our nation, which also affects our day-to-day existence and environment. The daily stressors of anxiety and fears and other debilitating issues are a result of the climate of the nation that we're living in. I can't emphasize enough the multi-dimensional approach and that we must recognize the power we possess.

Renée: You mentioned prayer and that is most critical. The Bible says to pray for those in authority so we can live a peaceable life (1Timothy 2:1-2). I was talking to someone about the current administration, and I said that I sometimes do more criticizing than praying. We have to use our spiritual weapon of prayer.

You said all the resources we need is in the House. I know in my church we've got licensed therapists, counselors, physicians, health care professionals, etc. I have even heard from some of them, especially the professional therapists who are licensed by the state, that they're not able to serve in a professional capacity due to a conflict of interests or the dual role issue. How do you reconcile that with the fact that they're skilled from a therapeutic standpoint and connect that to the spiritual gifts and ministry that God has given them? How do we connect those dots and get around that?

Dr. Rob: That can present itself as a challenge. However, it has to be treated like any other professional relationship. As a clinician, for example, the altar is a place where we can pray for you, but it's not a place where I write you a prescription. With that being said, I think it will vary from individual to individual as to how they see their role, their gifts, being utilized in the church apart from their professional capacity. For example, at our church, we do have licensed professional counselors who will give of their time by providing so many sessions to members of the congregation, but beyond that, they have to enter into a professional agreement. And it can be somewhat challenging for someone at the altar who has shared intimate details of their life, but with maturity, we can navigate through those situations and make sure everyone is comfortable and at peace with it. It's a judgment free zone, and no one is going to be critiqued or judged based on the professional relationship that we might have outside of our fellowship as brothers and sisters in Christ.

FAMILY DYNAMICS AND HEALTH

Renée: As doctors, when you come to your office, especially as a new patient, there is paperwork to fill out. Part of the paperwork is providing our family medical history, mother, father, siblings, etc. on both sides of your family. You ask for a comprehensive history of who suffered with diseases and disorders such as cancer, diabetes, high blood pressure, mental illness, and others. I'm asking an obvious question, but why is that so important when you're diagnosing or treating me as a patient?

Dr. Karla: That's a great question. We see generational issues. We can talk about it from the spiritual and the natural. We see cycles being repeated of spiritual, emotional, physical attacks. If we know what Grandma was dealing with, we're better equipped to, first of all, catch it before it manifests; we're able to say that if Grandma was battling diabetes, then it's an attack that's in your bloodline. So before you even have any symptoms of diabetes, we know it's important for you to exercise, manage your weight, and have the proper diet to prevent being susceptible to those things we know attacked your bloodline. It also helps with treating you; if you come in with symptoms of something and we know this has been in your family, we're more likely to zero right in and be able to make sure this isn't going on. It helps with regards to prevention in the now, as well as from a treatment standpoint in moving forward in knowing what we're fighting to get to the ultimate place of healing. It goes right back to having that open dialogue that many of us particularly in our community don't have, as it relates to what's going on with us and our family with our mental and physical health. Some of these issues are taboo and we just won't talk about it. This seems to be an area where the enemy tries to prevail. So if we're not talking, the enemy is constantly trying to have the upper hand, yet we know we have the tools to have divine health. That is a great question that as the church (particularly in our community and in our culture), we really need to embrace, and that is talking more about our history.

Dr. Rob: In addition to what Dr. Karla said about knowing what to look out for and what lifestyle adjustments need to be made, but knowing what to pray *against*, as believers, as physicians, as professionals, we truly believe and understand that these generational attacks that the enemy is trying to send our way as it relates to our health are things that if we're aware of and pray against, we can have the victory over. But if we stay in silence and don't have that dialogue, that conversation, it gives the enemy to opportunity to creep in with disease and illness. Because of the lack of those conversations, we didn't know to pray against the cancer that not only Grandma had, but Mama had, her brothers, and sisters had.

Renée: That is such a challenge with our community. I just had a conversation recently where the family didn't talk about it. "What goes on in this house, stays in this house." It was taboo to even speak about certain things, although it would help us tremendously if we knew that Great Grandpa was an alcoholic or that he was abusive. We'll use the term "generational curses," but what do we do about it? I like to say "generational behaviors" when it comes to the believer because if you're a believer, you're no longer cursed. But I do understand what we're saying when we use "generational curses." It would help to find out about Aunt so and so, and how she would erupt in anger over seemingly nothing and was such a bitter woman. Why was she bitter? Uncle or Cousin may give you a hint, but even if you don't know why, it helps to understand why her daughter is bitter, angry, hates men, etc.

Silence is such an enemy and a tactic of the enemy. He shoots his best shot with that one.

Renée: Can you share a particular instance when Rob and Karla and the family had a challenge, and you had to take some of your own medicine?

Dr. Rob: Interesting how God works, because this ministry, Urban Housecall, was birthed out of that type of moment where ours was a story of living in sickness, accepting it as our norm, and not recognizing that God desired more and had better for us. Our testimony is that we were living with diabetes, high blood pressure, high cholesterol, being obese, and overweight. We were and are clinicians living through this, but not recognizing that God had so much more for us. It was a moment of clarity, a season of fasting and prayer when He spoke to us and said, "This isn't My best for you." Dr. Karla was taking four insulin shots a day for diabetes. She actually said to God, "I don't want to do this anymore." God responded, "I don't want for you to, nor was it My plan for you do this, ever." It was that moment of clarity where we began to see our role in our sicknesses and physical disease we were living in where He showed us how to transition into health.

I flipped your question—we took the medicine first, and then it birthed this ministry is how we got to the place we are now.

On a continual basis, we have to be reminded or remind ourselves, whether it's related to our physical health, spiritual health, emotional health, we've never arrived, we can always do better, and strive to be better. We are very honest with ourselves in that, and try as best as we can to continually improve upon what it is that is our here and now or our "status quo" for the moment.

Renée: Dr. Karla, in another conversation that you and I had, you mentioned the term "grace place" that God gives all believers. What does that mean? How does that relate to those who have been given the "privilege" of caring for the souls of others? We're concerned with their health because in order to dispense health and good quality care, you have to be much up on your health, not perfect, but at least willing to go there and address things and take care of yourself so you can take care of others.

Dr. Karla: I believe when God creates each one of us and our giftings, the plan and purpose for our lives, He also creates us with a measure of grace to walk that out. The anointing that He gives you to go about your journey, whatever that may be, whatever He created you to do to carry out His agenda, He's going to give you the grace to do it. That's why people look around at someone else and say, "How did you do that?" We've had those moments where we asked ourselves, "How in the world did we do that, with four children, working full time jobs? How did we accomplish that?" It's only by His grace. That's the "grace place." He gives you exactly what you need to thrive and accomplish the very goal that He's purposed to accomplish. This is something that He gives us all, and that's why we have to be so careful of not being envious of someone else's anointing or giftings or talents, because you weren't graced for that. He graced you for what He desires you to do and that's **your** *grace place, your sweet spot*, where you're most effective. That's where you're breaking the chains of bondage of those He places in your path. It's something we all have, and so often we might think of ourselves as a victim, but that's a part of the grace He gives us to go through what we have to go through. In doing so, we're able to use that testimony to free others. As it relates to the privilege of caring for the souls of others, you're graced for that. Not everyone is called to be a pastor, a chaplain, or a grief counselor. There's a certain measure of grace that you have to have to walk in the largeness of being a soul care giver. The largeness, the burden, the weight of it all and the only way you can do it is to be graced for it.

Renée: I like how you put that. Recently, I was speaking with a group of ladies at a Bible study. We were given the opportunity to tell "your truth." Where are you right now? What is it you're going through, struggling with? Some didn't know what to do; others couldn't understand why they were going through it. It would have been good to have had those words, *grace place, sweet spot*...to paint a picture so that they could be a little more at ease, even with the stress and pain they were experiencing. To have told them, "You're graced for this" .... I will have the opportunity to share it in this framework again, even before this book comes out.

So with that said, with all that you do, how do you care for your own soul, take your own medicine as you care for others?

Dr. Rob: You're to give from a place of overflow. It's critical that we're constantly feeding ourselves, mind, body, and spirit that we're tending to our own needs and health. We're under a pastor who loves and cares for us. We make sure we're seeking their counsel, guidance, and wisdom as needed. And we certainly have to ensure that we are full, that we're not giving from a place of a deficit, because that's when everything starts to crumble. When you are required, whether by profession, calling, or assignment, to pour out to others and you're not ensuring that you're full, that's a problem. We must ensure that we're reading our Word, our Bible—that we're praying, surrounding ourselves with others who can pour into us, and that we can be accountable to. It's so important to know that we can call upon them when we need it instead of constantly being in the pouring out mode, but allowing ourselves to be filled. Another thing that can pose a problem for those who are used to being in the role of pouring into others is that they won't receive, even when offered to be filled.

We have to recognize as those who come to us to be filled are not prideful, yet we can be prideful. We have to ask for and seek out the very filling we need to be able to continue to pour from a place of overflow.

Renée: Being able to ask for help when you recognize you need it—I'm thinking in terms of pastors and other leaders, because the responsibility is so great and you're constantly giving out. Whose responsibility is it for the pastor's health, the holistic health of that pastor? Is it correct to say that it rests with that pastor?

Both: Absolutely!

Renée: Sometimes you may see that a pastor might be struggling with a particular area, and you discern that. One of the charges of a leadership team is to hold up the arms of the pastor. What should the associate ministers, ministry leaders, elders, deacons, teachers (whatever your organizational structure) do to help?

Dr. Rob: We should be interceding continually for our pastors. Particularly as leaders, we should have an understanding as to the weight of ministry. Even in our respective leadership roles, regardless of the organizational structure of your church, you know the weight that you're carrying as a leader and that weight is increased many-fold for the pastor. As leaders, we must intercede for our pastors.

Our pastor always says that he has a pastor. There should be someone in addition to the church leadership that they can go to. Certainly, they should surround themselves with other pastors. But as leaders, we should be praying for them daily, should be at the top of our priority and prayer list alongside our family—they need to be right at the top. They have the lives and souls for so many people they are responsible to God for. That's a heavy weight, an assignment that they accepted, but even in acceptance, it doesn't mean it's any less burdensome.

Dr. Karla: Our pastor always says if we're in a leadership meeting, "I wouldn't have you in this room if I didn't trust you." Having people around you that you can trust that you can receive wisdom from, Christian critique from, that you can say, "You don't look well. What's going on with you?"—That's where good leadership comes in, when you have good people around you that can speak honestly to you. Ask those questions—Have you been to the doctor lately? You need to take a break, etc. I think about Galatians 6:9, "Let's not be weary in well doing." We forget sometimes that we can be so busy "doing" church that we can miss some of the important signs that our spiritual, emotional, or physical health is suffering or crumbling because we're so busy "doing." Having those people around you that you can receive from and as Dr. Rob said, those people that you are accountable to. Having your own pastor or other leaders you can be accountable to is going to be key.

Renée: You've written a book, *In Sickness and In Health,* that gives couples insight into how to live their best and healthiest lives. This is so critical because the family and marriage is under such a terrific attack today as the world insists on redefining the family and the high incidence of divorce, even in Christian households. I understand that some marriages just cannot be saved. A great concern, however, is the watershed effect on the children. What advice do you give to couples in ministry—for example, the pastor, their spouse, spiritual leaders, and their spouse? What can we have in place that will help maintain and safeguard an emotionally healthy marriage and family with or without children?

Dr. Rob: It's important to recognize that no matter how large your ministerial assignment is, your first ministry is your family. 1 Timothy 3:5 refers to those who seek to be a leader in the church should first be a leader in their home. We must take the time to recognize what's important to our family and invest in those areas. The only way those children will respect you is if you've taken the time in identifying what's important to them. Prioritizing them and seeing to it that their needs are met. Having Daddy and Mommy time with kids and having Daddy and Mommy time without the kids so that the spouse feels they are a priority. Also recognize that just because I knew what was important to you five years ago doesn't mean that's the same thing important to you today. Having those frequent check ins to maintain the health of the relationship and remind the spouse and children that they remain a priority above all else is important.

Renée: As Dr. Karla mentioned, we can get so busy "doing" church, especially when you're in leadership. You have this meeting and that meeting and all of this going on. Because the pastor knows firsthand what needs to get done, I think it's important that the pastor also emphasizes healthy marriages and families. We might have that emphasis as part of our mission or vision statement, and that's good, but actualizing it is another thing. For example, the pastor may say, "Bro. or Sis. _____, I'm going to excuse you from this meeting." It's a challenge when folks don't show up when they said they would. You may tend to overwork those volunteers who are showing up, but you're creating a situation at home with your leaders and volunteers that's not healthy. That balance is so important.

Can you give me a basic definition of a healthy soul care provider or soul care giver in today's church or Christian community?

Dr. Karla: A healthy soul care provider is someone who is pouring out from a place of abundance, overflow—a place of health and healing that bubbles over to free the lives and souls of those that they are charged with and caring for. One of the healthiest ways to lead is by example. If you're practicing the lifestyle of health in mind, body, and spirit, you're modeling that for those you're caring for. In doing so, you're able to ensure that you're constantly in a state of being refilled, poured into to maintain your own health.

Renée: A place of honesty?

Dr. Karla: Absolutely, because I have to know when I'm not at that place of overflow or I don't have in place what I need to be refilled.

Renée: I need to know when I have to take some time off. Sometimes there's a fear that things just can't run unless you're there. Well if you're there and, well, let's be plain, you're "jacked up," things will not run well.

Dr. Karla: That's another sign of a good leader, someone who is raising up others to be able to function in your absence because we know it's not about one person. This Kingdom work is about advancing God's agenda. It can't ever be about one person so that our eyes are on the much larger vision and agenda at hand. A good leader will make sure that things are running effectively, whether they're physically present or not.

Renée: It's God's church. He has graced us to join Him in this good work.

Dr. Karla: This is a marathon and not a sprint. We think about being healed as a one-stop thing, and it's not. There's maintenance and continual steps you have to take to live out and walk out your deliverance from whatever it may be. The enemy is always seeking an opportunity to re-occupy, so we must continually remind him that this is not your home; you have no place here. It's a continual journey that we're on to maintain. We're either at a spot to achieve divine health, reclaim divine health, or maintain diving health. We can all fall into one of those three categories. It's a wonderful reminder that our work is never done; we can always seek His hand in our emotional, physical, and spiritual health.

[END OF CONVERSATION]

Book and resources by the Robinsons:

In Sickness & In Health

www.urbanhousecall.com

Considerations?

_____

_____

_____

_____

_____

Confessions?

_____

_____

_____

_____

_____

Convictions?

_____

_____

_____

_____

_____

More Conversations?

_____

_____

_____

_____

_____

MEDITATIONAL SOUL NOTE

Why Art Thou Cast Down?

"Depression comes when we have *compressed* our view of God's ability and desire to help us, *suppressed* the memory of God's faithfulness to us in the past, and *repressed* our reverence, adoration and praise to God. Therefore, we continually express our dissatisfaction with life. We now must confess to God that our walk with him has been out of focus.

"Why are thou cast down, O my soul? Is the question David asked. In verses 1 and 2 he says the same way the deer is thirsty for water, I'm thirsty for God! Yet despite his hunger, David confesses in verse 3, that all he'd been eating was tears. Thirsty, wanting more of the fresh living water of God, but dieting on salt water tears. David's words were focused, but not his actions. David threw a party but only invited his tears. Have you ever thrown a party like that? But in verse 4 David says, "This party is over!" David says two key words that indicated that the dark cloud was lifting—"I Remember!" Part of our definition of depression is suppressing the memory of the goodness of God in times past. Suppression leads to depression. So to beat depression we have to remember."

–R. Carnell Jones, *Tekel Emotions in the Balance* , p. 109

PSALM 42:1-5

As the deer pants for the water brooks, So pants my soul for You, O God.

My soul thirsts for God, for the living God. When shall I come and appear before God?

My tears have been my food day and night. While they continually say to me, "Where is your God?"

When I remember these things, I pour out my soul within me. For I used to go with the multitude; I went with them to the house of God, With the voice of joy and praise, With a multitude that kept a pilgrim feast.

Why are you cast down, O my soul? And why are you disquieted within me? Hope in God, for I shall yet praise Him. For the help of His countenance.

CHAPTER 10

THE PASTOR'S WIFE– HER FEELINGS MATTER TOO!

Conversation with **Renita K. Hopkins**

RENITA K. HOPKINS was born in Fort Wayne, Indiana. Her spiritual life's anchor was rooted in the Christian family home in which she was raised. Although they are now deceased, her parents successfully instilled within her a Christian foundation she has continually built on to this day. She is the youngest in her family and has five loving and supportive siblings. While still residing in Fort Wayne, she met, fell in love with, and married her soulmate, Gary L. Hopkins. They have been married for thirty-three years, and were truly blessed as parents twenty-one years ago with the birth of their wonderful son, JaVon.

She accepted Jesus as her Lord and Savior as a young child. At the age of twenty-five, she then dedicated her life as a Christian to the will and service of God. She is committed to being an active leader in the church and has developed and served in various ministries (Gate Keeper/Usher, Youth Leader and Overseer, Women's Leader, Pastor's Aid, Trustee and Office of Administration). Over the span of their marriage, she and her husband have been on a spiritual journey. While residing in Memphis, Tennessee, her husband accepted his call into the ministry in 1996. Being obedient to God's instructions, they then relocated to Charlotte, North Carolina, and founded their church ministry (Whole Armor Christian Life Center) in 2007. As pastor and wife, they celebrated their eleventh year church anniversary in July 2018.

In preparation for serving in the ministry, God strategically aligned and advanced her professional career path. She was accepted into the University of Indianapolis Nursing Program and graduated in 1983. Upon successfully passing her State Board's Exam, she was licensed as a Registered Nurse. Although she initially worked in the clinical areas of Orthopedics and Pediatric Cardiology, she was spiritually led to specialize in the field of Psychiatric and Mental Health Nursing. Over the past thirty-five years, she enhanced her clinical experience and diversified her nursing resume to include all levels of behavioral health patient care (inpatient and outpatient), utilization review and regulatory compliance, nursing administration and corporate nurse consultant in the opening of psychiatric emergency room services, and four psychiatric hospitals in the states of Tennessee and North Carolina.

[BEGINNING OF CONVERSATION]

Renée: How long have you been a pastor's wife?

Renita: My husband and I have been married for thirty-three years and in the ministry for twenty-two years. As pastor's wife of the church ministry we founded (Whole Armor Christian

Life Center), we were blessed in celebrating this past July 2018 our eleventh year church anniversary.

Renée: Were you surprised at his calling to pastor?

Renita K. Hopkins

Renita: Not really. When we were dating and living in Ft. Wayne, Indiana, Gary was very active in the church as a young man. He was close to his uncle, who was the pastor of the church he was raised in, and served as his right hand. I always heard from family and friends who knew Gary quite well that one day he would be a pastor. I heard it but dismissed it at the same time. When it evolved, I guess I had subconsciously prepared myself based on what people had told me and his endless dedication to serving in the church. Leading up to the acceptance of being called into the ministry, God took us through an amazing experience together. This experience confirmed the spiritual calling upon the life of my spouse directly from God Almighty. From that same spiritual experience we shared together, I too received a direct revelation from God. That experience taught me that this was not just a sole call for Gary into the ministry, but a call upon us both.

Renée: Will you share that experience?

Renita: When we lived in Memphis, Tennessee, my husband was required to travel extensively for work and would be gone from home at least two to three weeks out of the month. I then had conditioned myself to being at home alone. My routine each night before settling into bed was securing the house by locking up and closing all blinds. It was imperative that the blinds on our bedroom's French doors were closed tightly to prevent the big night light in the backyard from shining through.

This particular time when Gary came back from his travels, instead of coming home with a new pair of shoes as he always did, he had come home with various Bibles and theology books he had purchased. This was very different, because he used to have a shoe fetish, and to every city he traveled, he made it a point to go out and shop for another pair of new shoes. He could not explain how or why on this occasion he set out on a shoe excursion, but instead found himself shopping in a Christian bookstore.

That night when he came back home, when we went to bed, we were both awakened in a startle by similar dreams of fire. In attempt to return to sleep, my eyes were closed, but I could feel this bright light in the room. I told Gary that he hadn't turned off the hall light. He said that he did. I then said, "Well, cut off the overhead light." He said, "Renita, all the lights are out." I said, "Well then, change the direction of blinds because the night light is coming through." Neither he nor I could determine where this light was coming from and because the light was so bright, it would not allow us to go back to sleep. We said, "What is that light?" Above our head was this gleaming, glowing light. It was from God. The coffered ceiling even showed the different radiant dimensions of light. It was like Moses seeing the burning bush.

We wondered, "What is that?" Gary said he knew what it was. He quietly got up and went to the front of the house into the family room. That's when he and God had their talk and he accepted his call. My husband had this thing when he had to tell me something that was really important. If I was in the bedroom, he would come into the room, lean on the dresser, and say, "We have to talk." That night, when he came back to the bedroom, he positioned himself by the dresser and said, "We have to talk." I already knew. That's when he said, "I've accepted my calling." I said, "I know. The light that He showed us both was God saying that we both have a calling. You're not in this alone."

There is a huge difference between a couple learning after marriage that their spouse would be accepting his or her calling into the ministry versus a couple making the choice to marry clearly knowing in advance one or both of them had already accepted their call into the ministry.

This was something that was going to be a lifestyle change for both of us. I'm glad God showed us both with that experience. It helped me to see and say to God, "I guess I'm a part of this too!"

Renée: That is so interesting how God showed you both at the same time and how you were called at the same time, as opposed to someone who is marrying a pastor and it's brand new.

Renita: With marrying into the ministry, you have some knowledge base as to what type of lifestyle you're walking into, and what ministry role you are choosing to accept. But if you're married already, and you have this binding union for better or for worse, you know that this is something you have to accept if you are truly destined to keep your marital vows. So do you really have a choice?

Renée: I can imagine when you talk to others who are already married, they may say, "I didn't sign up for this." How do you encourage those who may not be as accepting of their husband's call as you were?

Renita: Now acceptance is one thing, but then the lifestyle changes that come with it are something else.

Renée: Sounds like a process.

Renita: Yes, you're right. My "total" acceptance of being in the ministry was indeed a process. The calling on my husband's life did affect me. Even though I knew what God was asking of him and we're walking in this ministry together, it was still a transition for both of us. Although we weren't these hard-core party people, ministry did and has changed the dynamics of our home and daily lifestyles. We still strived to maintain yet balance our charismatic personalities of being open, friendly, and hospitable. The big change for me was learning that I had to now share my spouse and have the willingness to do so. Before the ministry, we had time and opportunity to spend endless hours together and weekend date nights. Now with our bi-vocational work schedules, continuous availability to others, Saturdays designated to preparation for Sunday, and Sunday church services, our quality time solely together is truly limited. I no longer have that one hundred percent attention of my husband. I have to be even more in tune with God to know that when He is requiring my husband's full attention and however long it takes, I must be willing and able to step aside. My husband and others frequently say that I am spoiled rotten because I was the baby in my family, and therefore he had to continue what he had inherited. Before the birth of our son (JaVon), for twelve years, it was just Gary and me. Even though God was always a part of our marriage, I've truly learned over the years how to share my husband's time and attention for the spiritual benefit of others.

Renée: You were no longer the number one focal point in his life. He spoiled you. You had grown to expect certain things from him, right?

Renita: Lifestyle adjustments with even the simplest of things that we had grown accustomed to—once he became a pastor, a simple thing such as trying to take a vacation became tedious trying to work around ministry schedules and weekends being dedicated to Sunday church services.

Renée: Are you still making those adjustments?

Renita: Yes, continuously, depending on the situation, needs of the ministry, and/or specific needs of a member within the congregation. What you thought were your plans are now subject to being placed on hold, pushed temporarily to the side, and even canceled.

Renée: When a church member needs counseling, do they insist, "I need to talk to Pastor," or because they know you're a psychiatric nurse and do counseling, does it matter?

Renita: The ministry counseling we offer is based on biblical doctrine and is conducted by the two of us together. Our counseling targets individual, marriage, and family. However, with direct women issues if required, I will conduct one-on-one counseling, and he does the same for men.

Renée: What is the size of your ministry?

Renita: Our congregation is small with forty to fifty members.

Renée: So you can do that now rather easily. As you grow, that may change.

Renita: In a small church, direct counseling from the pastor and his wife can have its positive and negative effects. It is a positive opportunity to build a closer bond with your members, while being instrumental in helping them find resolution of their concerns. But as the ministry grows, so too does the influx of issues. It becomes a juggling act to continue providing the same one-on-one support so that you don't overlook anyone's issues. Not only is it challenging, it can be overbearing to try to avoid the negative effects a member might experience if they feel their issues have been slighted. They could become hurt and/or disconnected from the church. In larger churches, pastors are able to provide various counseling ministries to effectively reach the needs of their congregations. But right now, with the size of our church, prayerfully we're taking it on ourselves.

Renée: Are you preparing for when you will no longer be able to do that? Have you thought about it?

Renita: Yes, we have. Within the structure of our church, we have a designated elder. On our spiritual organization chart, the elder is next in line to the pastor. We are also blessed that our elder happens to be married to one of the ministers in the church. As we've grown, they have become our right hand. They are spiritually equipped and available to step in and assist. We are a good team because they are in agreement with Pastor's vision for our church and willing to walk it out with us. As pastor, Gary also ministers in training classes in order to successfully educate, train, and ordain all incoming ministers. Once ordained, these ministers will be given added leadership responsibilities to assist too in the spiritual growth and development of the church.

Renée: And then you'll get the congregation ready for that transition.

Renita: Transition calls for change, and change for some is not always easy. Therefore, it is imperative we lead this ministry to be one that is forever growing and evolving so that our congregation does not settle into a spiritual comfort zone.

What we have learned in the process of ministry is this: in order for our congregation to accept transition with growth, we too must be able to delegate and set healthy boundaries and expectations.

Renée: How does your skill as a psychiatric nurse enhance your ministry?

Renita: I love this question! I've been a psychiatric nurse for almost thirty-five years. Once I made the career decision to specialize in the field of mental health, God then allowed my career path to flourish. After getting married and relocating to New Orleans, Louisiana, I was blessed with the ability to launch my career path working at Tulane Medical Center, which was a forerunner in the country of mental health and psychiatric innovations and treatments. I was able to learn all facets while working directly with child, adolescent, adult, and geriatric populations. I was also able to advance my nursing skill set in working with substance abuse patients requiring detox and addiction recovery. I continually had, over the years of my career, this internal drive to advance in all areas of mental health nursing. Every job I acquired allowed me to successfully build my nursing resume to include all levels of behavioral health patient care (inpatient and outpatient), utilization review, nursing administration, corporate nurse consultant in the opening of psychiatric emergency room services, and four psychiatric hospitals in the states of Tennessee and North Carolina.

Once Gary went into the ministry and became a pastor, a light bulb came on confirming as to why God had anchored my nursing career path in the field of mental health. It was because I was about to embark on a spiritual journey that would require me as a pastor's wife to be educated and effectively equipped to help those in need holistically (spiritually, mentally and physically). Wow—it's so amazing and such a blessing to actually know my personal ministry motto, "helping those who cannot help themselves" truly aligns with the call GOD has upon my life—Amen!

Renée: What a gift!

Renita: I now have the ability to be able to look at someone, discern, and ask, "Are you okay?" I can look at someone's family dynamics and ask if they need help. My professional career path was vital in preparing me for the ministry.

Renée: And the Holy Spirit gives you that discernment.

Renita: Exactly! When I was young and fresh out of nursing school, I sought out to become a pediatric cardiology nurse, because I loved children and wanted to make an impact in nursing them back to good health. But one Sunday, our unit's census dropped, requiring all staff nurses being pulled to work in different areas of the hospital. Well I got pulled to the eighth floor, which was mental health, and I went kicking and screaming. But to my surprise, once I got up there, I loved it! I did not recognize it at the time, but the Holy Spirit was telling me then that this is where I need to be.

Renée: Today, it seems there is an escalation of mental illness—or is it that we're now seeing so much more of it?

Renita: It's more of awareness. It's always been there, but we've dismissed it for other things or refused to accept the sickness for what it really is, especially in the black community and the black church. It's a taboo subject, but as time has evolved, treatment for the mentally ill has become more readily available for all. The black community as a whole is now becoming more enlightened and knowledgeable in the areas of mental illness. Awareness has grown, but there's still a lot of work to do in the area of acceptance.

Renée: You all have a unique situation, because when a family has a mental illness, you're able to guide them and meet the need. How would you advise the church that doesn't have a "Renita Hopkins" or resources in place to deal with it?

Renita: Most importantly, the church leadership has to be open and willing to address their congregation holistically. If a mental health issue arises within the church, and it will, don't dismiss it! If there are no mental health professionals within the church to take on this ministry, it is imperative to gather all available resources within and/or outside of the church to provide support and offer treatment options as quickly as possible. To avoid or delay a person receiving the mental health services they need can sometimes become a matter of life or death. All churches should have a Mental Health and Substance Abuse Resource Manual that is accessible and contains all local hospitals with available emergency services, community listings of the various levels of treatment, and qualified professional clinicians with contact numbers and hours of operation. When members of your congregation with mental health issues can feel open and safe to disclose without the repercussions of being judged or viewed as weird or crazy, they will then be more apt to ask for help.

Renée: Most churches do have the resources in the House (their church) if they look deep enough—in addition to the pastor's being one hundred percent committed to first recognize that there are those in the church who are suffering, and then willing to provide the help and resources. Of course, there is the issue of professional protocol in a ministry setting being adhered to.

Renita: As a mental health professional, maintaining confidentiality and healthy boundaries must always be taken into consideration. If they are not able to directly intervene, they do have the clinical skill set to assist in making the appropriate referrals.

Renée: Communication is important. While it is critical that help is in place, the whole congregation must be made aware and educated about mental health and the substance abuse resources available. We also have to help people to not be ashamed to admit they need help.

Renita: Establishing trust is the gateway to effective and healthy communication. As previously stated, open communication addressing the reality of mental health has to start with the pastor and leadership team of the church. In the world we live today, mental health issues, addiction, and even suicide is expanding rapidly through all walks of life. Seeking out all communication opportunities to increase awareness and educate is the key.

Renée: So how do you, Renita Hopkins, care for yourself?

Renita: Because I am bi-vocational, meaning my profession as a mental health nurse Monday through Friday and my spiritual ministry 24/7, I have learned that I have to have my own quiet time. Despite how full my daily schedule can be, for my holistic wellbeing, I make a conscious effort to look out for just me. It may be spending one-on-one with God, relaxing in the bed, sitting on the front porch, or just watching my favorite television shows. It's my time. I'm a big advocate of massages. Body massages with aromatherapy allow me to destress and rejuvenate from the mental drain of my profession and the physical drain of the ministry.

I appreciate that my husband and son are both in tune to when I am in a "me zone" and respectfully give me that time without interruption. That is a blessing!

Renée: Maintenance is so essential to overall health.

Renita: Learning to create a lifestyle that allows a healthy emotional balance for your spouse, your family, your ministry and not forgetting about self is, indeed, the key.

Renée: You've got to take care of self. Some women even feel guilty doing that and see it in a negative lens of self-indulgence. I listen to women in ministry and pastors' wives who even tell me that. Recently, I was in Washington, DC for an event called Deborah's Voice. While there, I had a moment to engage with a pastor's wife. She looked relaxed and shared that the weekend was "down time" for her. Even though she was a part of a ministry team there, it was still a time to rest and be rejuvenated. Our conversation was interrupted with a phone call from home where she was giving step-by-step instructions for something that had she been there, she would have easily handled herself. After the call ended, we talked specifically about her self-care, and she agreed how important it was, but added there is that tinge of guilt when you do. Not that she was aggravated by the need to respond to the call from home, because she did so with patience and love—it just emphasized and validated the need for intentional self-care.

Renita: That is definitely something I had to learn, unfortunately the hard way. It took years to learn. Two years before Gary and I had our son (JaVon), I had a miscarriage at eight months. That was so devastating to me that once JaVon did come, I put Renita on a shelf and I devoted my life to the wellbeing of my son, my husband, and the requirements of the ministry. I forgot about Renita and totally stopped caring for myself. The needs of Renita were never addressed or even came into play. After I had finally lost myself, at the same time, I found myself. I had become sad, sullen, and depressed. Not willing to fully accept the reality of my depression, (because I was a mental health nurse, and mental health nurses just don't get depressed), finally, my husband, who knew something was wrong, convinced me to schedule an appointment with my doctor.

Reluctantly, I went to the doctor, and as soon as he entered the exam room, I immediately broke down and began crying, boo-hoo-ing, and telling him, "My husband is saying I'm depressed. But I'm not depressed." The doctor patiently allowed me to cry it out, assessed my symptoms, and listened as I gave multiple reasons in attempt to convince him I was indeed not depressed. He then looked at me eye-to-eye, and said, "Renita, you are depressed." It was then I was diagnosed with latent postpartum depression. I was treated with an antidepressant for approximately six months to a year and responded well. Praise God!

Renée: You lost yourself. Were you in a state of depression right after your first baby died?

Renita: Not depression, but more so dealing with grief and loss. Intense prayer, supplication, and communing with God allowed my husband and me to navigate sadly but successfully through that life experience.

Renée: You had a life-altering event that pointed you to a place of finding Renita—to go and get her because she's not doing too well—and then to make sure I take care of her, better than what I've been doing.

Renita: To be honest, realizing that I'm no good to anyone if I'm not good to myself—although my life is a continual work in progress, I now personally know I must strive to be the best I can be in order to effectively help and support the ministry I serve.

Renée: What would you say to that woman whose husband has just started a church or she is new to this pastor's wife role and also new to this "first lady" title? What advice would you give her, because it seems there's no training for the pastor's wife, or is there?

Renita: At the same time my husband and other ministers within our church were in preparation and training for their ordination, our pastor's wife held training classes for the ministers' wives. What I did learn in those training classes did prove beneficial in having a fundamental knowledge base of duties and expectations once my husband became a pastor. The most important advice I could offer to a new pastor's wife is to find and maintain an emotional balance with the members of your congregation.

Renée: How do you do that? How do you process the pain of ministry and protect yourself from being hurt by the very people you help?

Renita: It's not easy. To openly love others allows you to be emotionally vulnerable.

Initially, as a pastor's wife, I assumed if I was genuinely nice and loving to a member, I too would receive the same reciprocal response. I quickly learned that is not always the case. People can be harsh in their words and actions. As the pastor's wife, you overhear, see, and are the first to receive the frustrations a member who may have issues with the pastor or within the church. There would be times I allowed the actions of others to bring me to tears. My husband had to teach me how not to carry my emotions on my sleeves. I had to learn to be able to love people but be stronger in myself to not allow everything people say to penetrate my heart.

Renée: It takes time, doesn't it?

Renita: Yes, it takes time and it's still a work in progress. I've grown in my spiritual gift of discernment to be open and willingly address issues of concern that are truly for the uplifting of God's Kingdom and to simply dismiss those that are not.

Renée: What I'm hearing is the importance of discernment and the time it takes to learn about people. I'm learning even more from you and other pastors' wives that you guys sometimes get the short end of the stick because of the expectations.

Renita: Yes, unfortunately in those instances, we as pastors' wives are viewed and targeted to be weak and less intimidating.

Renée: But you had to learn that. On another note, the title, how do you feel about the title, "First Lady"?

Renita: I had to grow into that the title of "First Lady." When my husband became pastor, out of respect, members would address me as the "First Lady," and I would quickly respond back with the request just to be called Sister Renita. It took time for me to grow into this role and learn what my position was within the church. As I grew and understood that people look to me for leadership, guidance, direction, and spiritual advisement, I realized then that I was more than just their sister. It's an honor, and I have accepted the role.

Being "First Lady" is hard work and so much more than just a title. It's definitely not glitz and glam. I look past the title, for what its real meaning is, which is to be there as the number one support for my husband while working with my husband to be the spiritual leaders God called us to be for the congregation we serve.

Renée: In talking with sisters who are pastors' wives, I've heard a little bit of their hearts about their positions. One whose husband just started a church doesn't want to be overwhelmed. She accepted his call. He came from a family of pastors, so she was not totally taken aback. Another who has been serving with her husband for some years now rejects the title altogether.

Renita: I can understand that. Whether new or old in the ministry, you will always speak to your congregation in truth, despite the consequences. That keeps you from getting overwhelmed and approached with ungodly mess. If a member requests spiritual advisement and direction from my husband, me, or us both, we speak the truth. If then the member becomes so angered to the point of leaving the church because we spoke to them in truth, that's okay—they can leave.

Renée: As the saying goes, you have to step to me correctly because I will step to you correctly—in love.

Renita: In love. We are held accountable to do what God has ordained us to do, and that is in love, speak the truth.

Renée: You mentioned honesty, being able to be honest, being authentic, and being as transparent as wisdom will allow. Let's also talk about expectations, because sometimes people can have unrealistic expectations of pastors and pastors' wives—communicating clearly those expectations both ways what members expect of you and what you expect of members.

Renita: When a new member joins the church, we as couple let them know our bi-vocational availability. We provide pastoral contact information and reiterate if they need us, despite the hour, to call us. Sometimes that call will require us to react immediately, assist if needed, or simply to spiritually guide and direct. Providing contact information also lets the member know if you are having issues of concern and choose not to inform us, we can't help if we don't know. This is how healthy boundaries are then established and maintained.

Renée: So that there is no ambiguity, they know. Another question pertaining to the health of the pastor from your point of view is how can the leadership help safeguard the emotional and mental health and wellness of the pastor?

Renita: That's huge, because members sometimes fail to recognize the role and 24/7 responsibilities of a pastor. When a pastor is being pulled at the same time in multiple directions, over time, he/she can be holistically impacted. As members of the church body, we all have to assist in keeping our pastors healthy. To do that, it is vital that the leadership team of the church be accepting and committed to the pastor's vision for the church. True commitment allows church leaders to be willing and available to step in and carry out the vision when the pastor may need to step back and focus elsewhere (even on self). When a pastor genuinely knows his/her leadership team is one hundred percent on board, their ability to delegate, release, and relax comes naturally, knowing he/she is not working the ministry alone.

Renée: Part of our leadership and ministerial training at Nations Ford included a book called *The Pastor's Heart.*

Renita: Yes. To have committed ministers and leaders in the church is so critical to the overall wellbeing of the pastor and pastor's wife.

Renée: And then insisting that they both take a sabbatical and get periodic periods of rest and relaxation.

Renita: Most definitely, we are so blessed to have leaders within our leadership team where we are confident in their ability to effectively step in when pastor and/or I are away.

Renée: Do you have a mentor or a counselor?

Renita: No. I do, however, receive ministerial support, guidance, and direction from my husband and the sister churches with which we are affiliated. The pastors and their wives are best friends to both Gary and me. When we get the opportunities to spend quality time together, it is truly a joyous occasion by all. It is also a spiritual opportunity to learn, share, and keep each other encouraged to stay the course, despite ministry obstacles we sometimes have to face. To have this type of trustworthy release outlet has been and will always be instrumental in keeping us refreshed and dedicated to the ministries we serve.

Renée: Before we go, you mentioned the spectrum of mental illness as to how it can present itself. It can either reveal itself as hyper religious or actual demon possession. When you see the demonic spirit, what do you do?

Renita: I immediately go into prayer of spiritual warfare—praying directly for release for the person who is under attack and for protection of those who may have come into contact, including members of the family and church, the pastor, as well as myself. I also will intervene professionally if mental health safety and acute stabilization is required. Again, I praise God every day for the gift of discernment, because when the thin line between sanity and insanity is shown to me, there is immediate manifestation of continuous prayer that comes forth to help, but also to protect.

Renée: Continuous prayer, not giving up, even when we may get weary.

Renita: Not giving up because in the end, who is above all? Our dear Heavenly Father.

[END OF CONVERSATION]

Considerations?

_____
_____
_____
_____
_____
_____

Confessions?

_____
_____
_____
_____
_____
_____

Convictions?

_____
_____
_____
_____
_____
_____

More Conversations?

_____
_____
_____
_____
_____
_____

Oh, Lord! I lift my heart,
In gratitude, to Thee,
For blessings, manifold,
Thou hast bestowed on me.
When conflicts raged within,
Too blinding to express,
Thou pitied my still tongue,
And soothed my heart to rest.
Keep me within thy care;
Compel me, to the right;
'Tis sweet to walk with Thee,
In darkness or in light.

–"A Prayer" (1907) by Priscilla Jane Thompson, from *Conversations with God—Two Centuries of Prayers by African Americans,* James Melvin Washington, Ph.D., Editor

CHAPTER 11

THE BATTLE FOR A BETTER LOVE

Featuring excerpts from *A Different Kind of Happiness—Discovering the JOY That Comes from Sacrificial LOVE,* by **Dr. Larry Crabb**

D R. LARRY CRABB is a well-known psychologist, conference and seminar speaker, Bible teacher, popular author, and founder/director of New Way Ministries. He has served as scholar in residence at Colorado Christian University in Denver and visiting professor of spiritual formation for Richmont Graduate University in Atlanta. Dr. Crabb has been married to his wife, Rachael, for over fifty years. *(www. newwayministries.org)*

In my first conversation with Dr. Chand in 2007, he mentioned that years ago he was a student at Grace Theological

Seminary in Winona Lake, Indiana. While earning his Master's in Biblical Counseling, his mentor was Dr. Larry Crabb.

MORE THAN A SERVICE CALL

On his way from a service call in 2017, my son-in-law, a technician with a Charlotte cable company, sent me a picture of the front cover of a book. In his text he said that this book was a gift from one of his customers. While engaged in conversation, his customer learned that I was a grief recovery specialist and thought that perhaps his latest book would be of interest to me. As I looked closer, I was excited to see who had written it. Not getting it, I asked him who his customer was. He said, "The author!"

Dr. Larry Crabb has written several books, one of which is *A Different Kind of Happiness—Discovering the JOY That Comes from Sacrificial LOVE*. The appeal of the book is vast on so many levels. I find it to be a fitting conclusion for what we've been talking about. The title of the final chapter, "Life—Above and Under the Sun," was especially curious and brought to my mind a movie I had seen. You see, I enjoy taking a line or a scene and applying it to a spiritual truth or a life lesson.

In this particular film, what began as a normal flight was interrupted suddenly by severe turbulence. The passengers were jolted from a state of calmness to calamity. The pilot, though an alcoholic, was extraordinarily adept at flying an airplane. Obviously not to be trusted with how he employed life skills, he proved to the terrified passengers and flight crew his ability to successfully quiet the loudly shaken plane and bring them to safety. The co-pilot, while not understanding, reluctantly obeyed the pilot's command to change the flight controls that would send the plane hurling past the accepted normal and safe speed. Wild-eyed, he looked at the pilot in disbelief as he explained why it seemed he was putting them in a greater harm's way. The plane vibrated violently and appeared ready to break apart at any moment. The hearts of all those on board were in the same condition—ready to break. He explained that in order to get to a calmer air space, he had to push through the "crappy" air.

The pilot took seriously the responsibility of the souls on board who had been entrusted to his care. Despite his voice of assurance making its way throughout the cabin to stay put and keep their seat belts securely fastened, the faces of the passengers told of the horror in their hearts. They obeyed, breath abated, hearts constricted. Could they believe him? Would they believe him? Should they believe him?

The indicators on the control panel signaled the pilot's decision to soar ferociously taking them higher and higher. He had embraced the situation at hand with a committed confidence not allowing what he saw or felt in the natural to obscure what he knew awaited. The plane cooperated piercing the not so friendly skies. All of a sudden, the aircraft seemed to glide into a calmer air space. The waiting sun silently peaked through the angry clouds with a brilliant welcome. Accompanied with a peace that defied logic and reasoning considering what they just experienced, all souls on board could now breathe easy, sit back and rest.

I *Confess* that like the frightened passengers, I get shaken by the sometimes unbearable turbulence of life. I hold my breath as fear grips my soul, convinced that this too will *not* pass. And then I'm *Convicted* by the Voice of the Master of Creation that resonates, making its way to every crevice of my being: "Why are you fearful, O you of little faith? Then He arose and rebuked the winds and the sea, and there was a great calm" (Matthew 8:26). Still louder comes His still small Voice, cutting deeper: "O you of little faith, why did you doubt?" (Matthew 14:31).

I ask you to *Consider* some things Dr. Crabb expresses in *A Different Kind of Happiness*. It is impossible to summarize the book, so I encourage you to pick up a copy. I communicated with Dr. Crabb and told him about the book I was writing and how I wanted to quote some of his words. He was so gracious to offer whatever I wanted to share.

Winding down this leg of the journey, we are encouraged to shift our view of life from where we are right now—under the sun, to where we should be, *Confident* that God is taking us above the sun.

A PERSONAL BATTLE

As Dr. Crabb was writing the final chapter, "Life—Above and Under the Sun," he had received a message from his doctor with blood tests results. He was hurled into a fourth battle with cancer. A few weeks prior, he told how with a gentle nudge from heaven's "Spiritual Director", he read the book of Ecclesiastes. He didn't know it then, but with the news of the cancer returning, he realized that God was speaking to him through His Word where the writer is struggling to make sense of his life. King Solomon realizes that he can't hear from God, can't see or feel where God is even involved in this struggle.

Dr. Crabb went on to rehearse what the author who we believe to be Solomon or a sage who reported Solomon's thinking, lamented in Ecclesiastes.

The words of the Preacher, the son of David, king in Jerusalem.

"Vanity of vanities," says the Preacher: "Vanity of vanities, all is vanity."

I, the Preacher, was king over Israel in Jerusalem.

And I set my heart to seek and search out by wisdom concerning all that is done under heaven, this burdensome task God has given to the sons of man by which they may be exercised.

I have seen all the works that are done under the sun, and indeed, all is vanity and grasping for the wind.

I communed with my heart, saying "Look, I have attained greatness, and have gained more wisdom than all who were before me in Jerusalem. My heart has understood great wisdom and knowledge."

And I set my heart to know wisdom and to know madness and folly. I perceived that this also is grasping for the wind. For in much wisdom is much grief, And he who increases knowledge increases sorrow" (Ecclesiastes 1: 1-2; 12-18, NKJV).

THE ROAD TO A BETTER LOVE

Taking care of our own souls is quite the task. It is work, albeit a good work. It begins with a continuous shifting of our view of God and of ourselves until we are calm, still and rested enough to see clearly where we're headed. We often use the term "journey" as a way of describing this life. Earlier in my Introduction, I mentioned, a trek called the inward journey of the soul that is oftentimes reluctantly traveled. Dr. Larry Crabb refers to it as the *narrow road*. Once committed to the *narrow road*, the "battle for a better love" ensues.

This better love is one that originates from God alone and keeps us alive, healthy and whole. Better because it's the only way to truly love. It's that love that outlives eternity. This "better love" insists on having ample room in our hearts to stretch out to touch the deepest, darkest corners of our souls so that God can make Himself quite at home. It is divinely relational and when given from a place of overflow, glorifies God. It's that love God speaks of when He tells us *to love your neighbor as you love yourself.*

This *better love* is tempered with the notion of something Dr. Crabb calls "first thing happiness". This is in stark contrast to "second thing happiness" which is the kind of happiness that exists only when life treats us well. It is a *different kind of happiness discovering the joy that comes from sacrificial love.*

The Bible admonishes in Colossians 3:2 to "Set your affection [mind] on things above, not on things on the earth. (KJV). To do that, consider what Dr. Crabb has to say in Chapter 22, "Life Above and Under the Sun".

This chapter begins with a quote by Michael A. Eaton from his book, *Ecclesiastes.*

"If our view of life goes no further than 'under the sun, all our endeavors will have an undertone of misery."

(Michael A. Eaton, *Ecclesiastes* [Downers Grove, IL: Inter-Varsity, 1983] p.57).

Dr. Crabb writes:

"It is one thing to believe in God as a supporting actor in the drama of our story... that begins at our birth and ends at our death. It is quite another to know ourselves to be small but significant actors in the eternal drama of God's story... that begins in eternity past, stretches out from Genesis 1:1 through Revelation 22:21, and continues as a dance of love into eternity future.

Under the sun is

Everything that can be experienced through our five senses and understood by human reason.

Everything that shapes the smaller story of our lives.

Above the sun is

Everything that can be seen only with Spirit-granted faith and known only through divine revelation.

Everything that shapes the larger story of God."

(Crabb, pp. 226-227)

Earlier in Part Three, "A Beautiful Story is Unfolding, Even in the Darkest Night", Dr. Crabb ventures into a conversation that he imagines God is having with us as we strive to live and love above the sun. God is asking if we can see the beauty in the story He is telling. We responded that we could a little, but only dimly. He cautions that we're still caught up in the smaller story. We're busy managing our lives so that we could have "second thing happiness".

Let's end with the rest of the conversation:

"The pleasure you feel when life goes your way keeps you from longing to see the beauty of My story.

But Jesus, I do want to see the larger story of Your self-sacrificing love... to tell Your story by how I relate to others. But too often I fail, sometimes badly.

You always fall short of the way I love. But failure, when recognized and confessed, is your opportunity to rest in the hope of My forgiving, empowering love.

I think I've only been sipping the living water of Your love. Will I ever drink so freely and fully that your kind of love will reliably flow out of me into others?

Keep walking the narrow road. My purpose for you will not fail." (Crabb, pp. 209-210)

Considerations?

_____
_____
_____
_____
_____
_____

Confessions?

_____
_____
_____
_____
_____

Convictions?

_____
_____
_____
_____
_____

More Conversations?

_____
_____
_____
_____
_____

"Life is a short and fevered rehearsal for a concert we cannot stay to give. Just when we appear to have attained some proficiency we are forced to lay our instruments down. There is simply not time enough to think, to become, to perform what the constitution of our natures indicates we are capable of. How completely satisfying to turn from our limitations to a God who has none. Eternal years lie in His heart. For Him time does not pass, it remains, and those who are in Christ share with Him all the riches of limitless time and endless years. God never hurries. There are no deadlines against which He must work. Only to know this is to quiet our spirits and relax our nerves."

—"God's Infinitude," from *The Knowledge of the Holy,* A. W. Tozer pp.46-47

CHAPTER 12

JESUS THE WONDERFUL SOUL CARE PROVIDER AND LOVER OF MY SOUL

For we do not have a High Priest who is unable to sympathize and understand our weaknesses and temptations, but One who has been tempted [knowing exactly how it feels to be human] in every respect as we are, yet without [committing any] sin (Hebrews 4:15, Amplified Bible [AMP]).

The following is an excerpt from the thesis: "The Biblical Counselor: A Healthy Profile of the Soul Care Provider in the 21st Century Church" by Renée Hill Carter

HEALTHY LEADERS POSSESS a balance between leading deliberately and serving with humility. Our picture of health comes from Jesus Christ. "Jesus deliberately took the role of a servant because he knew who He was and maintained His sense of leadership as He served. He served by leading; He led by serving. He did not cease to be the leader when He served. Counseling in the church is truly a serving ministry. A soul care provider is serving those whom he engages in such a relationship.

A healthy leader realizes his or her responsibility to the role of leadership and the fact that leadership is influence. Counseling involves making the right responses. "Responsibility is the capacity to capably and faithfully make the right responses within our sphere of influence. A responsible person has a sense of, 'I am capable for this work.' Of course, we all realize from time to time that we are doing something for which we do not feel we are an expert. But a responsible person has a sense of 'I am capable, I am trained, prepared or supported to do this. With the help of God and my brothers and sisters cooperation I can do it'. It is a sense of being capable." (Yoder, *Healthy Leaders*, p.58)

SELF-LOVE?

Remembering the lyrics to a song that was learned as a child in the church, "Jesus loves me this I know, for the Bible tells me so," gives the assurance of God's love. The question to be asked of the Christian Counselor is, "Do I love myself?" Jesus issues an edict, *"Love thy neighbor as thyself"* (Romans 13:9). The counsel that is given must emanate from a healthy love relationship that the Biblical counselor has not only with God but with themselves. How does one determine healthy self-love? The answer is found in a battery of questions that the Biblical Counselor must ask and honestly answer.

- Do I really believe that I am fearfully and wonderfully made?
- Do I allow others to define me based on what I do and not who I am?

- Do I self-condemn?
- Do I struggle to forgive myself for my sins?
- Do I sentence myself to death when I have already been made alive unto Christ Jesus?

If you answer, "Yes" to any of the above questions, then a trip to the Cross is in order. For the Bible says, that while we were yet sinners, Christ died for the ungodly. The onus of our value is not on us but on the redemptive work completed at the Cross by Jesus Christ. Not loving oneself is actually a rejection of Chris's love. God is love—love is God. To be effective and to love those you serve, a healthy identity of who you are and the acceptance of God's love is required. *If you love yourself, you'll take care of yourself.*

SELF-MASTERY—THE INWARD JOURNEY

"Jesus encourages us to take the inward journey, the journey of the heart. There are two journeys in life; the inward journey and the outward journey. Unfortunately, many people take the outward journey first. The outward journey is forced upon us by life, which we must take, ready or not. The inward journey is entirely voluntary. Some will choose to never take it" (Bruno, T., *Jesus Ph.D. Psychologist*, 2000, p. 4). Socrates, other early philosophers and mystics encouraged a self-knowledge which is constantly evolving. We have been encouraged to "know thyself" and "to thine own self, be true." The metamorphic pilgrimage of self-mastery challenges the counselor to an authenticity that is necessary for walking alongside a troubled soul.

Finally, Jesus Christ is the holistic model, psychologically and spiritually, who addresses the needs for our well-being. Look at Jesus—He offers wisdom and insights for the spiritual journey.

He provides a guide for a Health Assessment based on this list of qualities from Tom Bruno's book.

He is a good listener.

He loves people.

He is intuitive.

He focuses on solutions.

He believes in our ability to change our lives.

He is compassionate.

He loves unconditionally.

He teaches us to focus.

He was fully human, and had feelings and thoughts like we do.

He teaches us to ask for what we need.

He stresses accountability.

He is well-grounded.

He is psychologically healthy.

His actions and words are motivated by love.

He shows us the need for purpose in our lives.

He has a deep understanding of suffering.

References cited:

Jesus Ph.D. Psychologist by Tom Bruno.

"To us a Son is given; and the government will be upon His shoulder, and His name will be called Wonderful Counselor" (Isaiah 9:6).

"Come to Me all you who labor and are heavy laden, and I will give you rest (Matthew 11:28).

"The Love of God is one of the great realities of the universe, a pillar upon which the hope of the world rests. But it is a personal, intimate thing, too. God does not love populations, He loves people. He loves not masses, but men. He loves us all with a mighty love that has no beginning and can have no end."

"The Love of God," *The Knowledge of the Holy*, A.W. Tozer, p. 102

AFTERWORD

There is more to say, to write, to think, to do when it comes to the emotional health of the soul care provider. I pray that these conversations have accomplished what they set out to do, to incite us all onward and upward to a healthier spirit, soul, and body.

But before we go, there is one group in particular that I wanted to spend more time talking with. These women are sometimes overlooked but in essence are the backbone of service and support in soul care. Whether leaders in their career, ministry, service and community organizations, pastor's wives and other areas of influence, their impact is great. Sometimes taken for granted, their presence is most felt when deficient or absent altogether. Many serve in a male-dominated arena, yet their voices are being raised, and with that are challenges that affect them emotionally and mentally. I am thankful to those ladies I had coffee with, lunch with, shared phone calls, emails, and texts to hear their hearts when it comes to their emotional health and their feelings.

I was so moved as I listened, that I wanted to include more conversations in this writing. I even set up a date and time for a roundtable virtual discussion by phone. Thankfully, my husband in his wisdom suggested that was another book altogether and that I should "land the plane," so I canceled the "meeting." (Thank you Bill, because I could keep on writing.)

Another book? Maybe. If not me, then maybe you. Action, yes. Change in all of us for the better? Absolutely. For the love of God, I hope so!

On a broader note, I leave you with this final thought.

As the sickness of evil and hatred decimate our land, I encourage, no, I implore us all to resist, persist, insist, press, to get our hearts right in those areas where they need to be. As we witness and experience the turbulent and heinous acts of all types of abuse and assaults against human beings that take our breath away, we must place the oxygen mask of God's pure air of love over our faces first, and breathe in deeper than we've ever done before. We will then be able to securely help our neighbor and our children do the same before "all hope is gone." In our anemic souls, we must be transfused often with the blood of Jesus. We cannot allow fear to stifle and block faith from flowing freely through our veins. The life of His blood and the undeniable insistence of His love must continually permeate and inform our brain (mind), our heart (soul), and our body so that our spirit will be in perfect alignment with the Spirit of the living God.

The choice is ours, faith or fear, life or death, love or hate? Our neighbors, our children need us; they need us healthy; they need us whole; they need us focused on the things that matter most. The enemy of our souls continues to wield decisive and sinister blows that have no regard for places once considered without question to be safe places...the mall, restaurants, the movies, the workplace, schools, houses of worship...

Once thought to be the safest of places on earth are now targets of deadly and insidious acts of violence, leaving us traumatized, or worse, anesthetized. Our schools, Columbine; Parkland, Florida; San Diego, Texas, and too many more should not be on this growing list. Our Houses of Worship, four little girls at Sunday School in Birmingham, Alabama; worshippers at Bible study in Charleston, South Carolina; carnage on Sunday morning in Sutherland Springs, Texas; massacre at the Jewish synagogue in Pittsburgh; and too many more should not be on this growing list. Surely, I thought in my naiveté, evil would have respect and dare not cross the threshold of our children's schools and our Houses of Worship.

Today, as I complete my manuscript to send to my publisher, breaking news just ripped through social media and flashed across the TV screen about a shooting at a high school in Matthews, North Carolina, which is next door to Charlotte. A student died and another is in custody. Yesterday, on Sunday in Kentucky, two people were gunned down in a grocery store. Saturday the day before, eleven lives were murdered and others injured in a Pittsburgh synagogue.

Hear the voice of God in 1 Peter 4:17: *"For the time has come for judgment to begin at the house of God; and if it begins with us first, what will be the end of those who do not obey the gospel of God?"*

As soul care providers, we can safely conclude that love, real love, the sacrificial love of the One in whose image we are made, will ignite our hearts to look at those we serve with His eye and with a more discerning scrutiny of Grace. But first, we must look at ourselves through the lens of God's love, for He said to "love your neighbor *as yourself.*" You owe it to them and to you, all for His Glory (Rom. 13:8-9).

DARE TO LOVE...DARE TO LIVE

A multitude of experiences, deeds, good and not so.
Thoughts, fleeting and staged.
Heights, depths.

A series of heart rhythms
So painful at times
So joyful at times
So tumultuous as needing a steady hand to still the discord so
much a part of it being realized.

A dance of pleasure no one could define but God.
A dance of death to old things whose demise must be celebrated
in order to live again.
An orchestra of symphonic booms of unrelated events that
somehow manage to meet at the same place, at the same time
that only the Conductor could have known
That only the Composer could have written
That only Maestro God could blend to such an ecstasy of Truth.

And you think you understand Love.
Love is unrelenting.
Love is unforgiving in its pursuit of itself.

Of its need to be fulfilled and grow eternally.
Of its destiny found only in the eyes of God.

It doesn't quite look like what I was told.
It doesn't quite feel like what I felt at first.
It contains sorrows
It contains the reality of certain truths that one thought could
never be.
It takes from you...it must so that it can be free to have room to
show the truth of itself.

It's possible that it can't be defined.
It's probable that it can only be lived to be discovered bit by bit.
And then we'll know.

Dare to love...Dare to live.

"Now may the God of peace Himself sanctify you completely, and may your whole spirit, soul, and body be preserved blameless at the coming of our Lord Jesus Christ. He who calls you is faithful, who also will do it."

— 1 Thess. 5:23-24

BOOKS AND RESOURCES BY PARTICIPANTS

Carter, Renée Hill. *A Good Work Begun*. USA: Xulon Press, 2012.

Chand, Samuel R. *Leadership Pain—The Classroom for Growth*. Nashville: Thomas Nelson, 2015.

Crabb, Dr. Larry. *A Different Kind of Happiness—Discovering the JOY That comes from Sacrificial LOVE*. Grand Rapids: Baker Books.

Garnto, Rita K. *Simple Self-Care Saved Me! Superpowers Included*. USA: Prominence Publishing, 2018

Green, Kathy R. *Meet Me in the Valley*. USA: Redemption Press, 2018.

Johnson, Bishop Joey. *God is Greater Than Family Mess*. USA: Winepress Publishing, 2003.

Johnson, Bishop Joey. *The God Who Grieves*. USA: Xulon Press, 2016.

Johnson, Bishop Joey. *Grief A Biblical Pathway to God*. Dallas: Saint Paul Press, 2016.

Peacock, Barbara L. Psalm 119 Journal. USA: Called Ministry, 2016

Peacock, Barbara L. C.A.L.L.E.D. to Teach. USA: Called Ministry

Robinson III, Robert C. MD, and Robinson, Karla L. MD. *In Sickness & In Health.* USA, 2015.

BOOKS AND RESOURCES REFERENCED AND RECOMMENDED

Bruno, Tom. *Jesus PH.D Psychologist.* Gainesville: Bridge-Logos Publishers, 2000.

Calhoun, Adele Ahlberg, *Spiritual Disciplines Handbook— Practices That Transform Us,* Downers Grove: Intervarsity Press, 2015

Hemfelt, Dr. Robert, and Warren, Dr. Paul. *Kids Who Carry Our Pain-Breaking the Cycle of Codependency for the Next Generation.* Nashville: Thomas Nelson Publishers, 1990.

Nouwen, Henri J.M. *The Wounded Healer.* New York: Image Doubleday, 1972.

James, John W., and Russell Friedman. *The Grief Recovery Handbook, 20th Anniversary Expanded Edition.* New York: Harper Collins Publishers, 2009.

Jones, R. Carnell. *Tekel Emotions in the Balance.* USA, 2014.

Richards, E. Randolph, and O'Brien, Brandon, J. *Misreading Scripture With Western Eyes Removing Cultural Blinders to Better Understand the Bible.* Downers Grove: InterVarsity Press, 2012.

Tozer, A.W. *The Knowledge of the Holy.* USA: Bibliotech Press, 2016.

Washington, James Melvin, *Conversations With God.* New York: HarperCollins Publishers, 1994.

Wright, Dr. Henry W. *A More Excellent Way - Be In Health.* New Kensington: Whitaker House, 2009.

About the Author
RENÉE HILL CARTER

Renée Hill Carter is a writer, award winning author, minister, and inspirational speaker. For twenty years, she was Executive Coordinator to Senior Pastor, the late Bishop Phillip M. Davis, Nations Ford Community Church. Gifted in the areas of teaching and encouraging, she is certified as a Grief Recovery Method® Specialist.

Renée has written for Lifeway Christian Resources (Lifeway.com). She wrote a student and leader lesson for the *YOU Adult Bible Study* curriculum and several daily readings. Numerous articles have been featured in the *Mature Living* magazine.

She is the author of the awarding winning book, *A Good Work Begun,* and has produced a two-set CD, *Soothing Touch: A Spa for Your Soul,* which is relaxing instrumental hymns and the timeless truth of the Psalms spoken by her soothing voice.

A graduate of Hampton University, Hampton, Virginia, and member of Delta Sigma Theta Sorority, she also received a Master of Arts degree in Christian Counseling from Queen City Bible College which functioned from 1993 until its closure in 2014. She teaches Effective Writing & Communications at The Envision Life School of Ministry and Leadership, Charlotte, NC.

Renée is a native of Beckley, West Virginia. She and her husband William (Bill) reside in Charlotte, North Carolina, and are the proud parents of three adult children, one grandson, and one granddaughter.

• • •

For more information, or to order additional copies of this book visit ReneeHillCarter.com.

CPSIA information can be obtained
at www.ICGtesting.com
Printed in the USA
FSHW011938090319